Sin,
Man,
and
the Grace of God

by

Michael W. Freitag

ISBN 978-1-64258-430-1 (paperback)
ISBN 978-1-64258-431-8 (digital)

Christian Faith Publishing, Inc.
832 Park Avenue
Meadville, PA 16335
www.christianfaithpublishing.com

Printed in the United States of America

Contents

Bible Key

I used several different Bible translations when quoting Bible verses. My purpose in doing that was to help people resist the urge to say, "That's not the Bible I use." I'm sure there are more translations, but the five I picked are listed below with their corresponding acronyms. The first four are the most commonly used in the United States, while the fifth is the translation used in the Fellowship of Christian Athletes Coach's Bible that I have been using lately. I apologize to the King-James-or-nothing crowd, but this book is intended to be easily read and understood by anyone, Christian and non-Christian alike. I used King James as much as I could when the meaning of the verse wasn't too abstract, which turned out to be not very often. When you compare verses of Scripture in the various translations, you find that they are worded differently, often dramatically so, but they end up saying essentially the same thing. I picked the translation I wanted to use because I liked the way it was worded for the topic that I was talking about. To counter my bias, I recommend that you cross-reference various translations on your own as you go through the book.

KJV - King James Version
NIV - New International Version
NASB - New American Standard Bible
NLT - New Living Translation
HCSB - Holman Christian Standard Bible

Preface

I am not a biblical scholar. This book is not written as a means to allow me to fill you with my knowledge and understanding of God's Word. The purpose of the book is to stimulate deep thinking and to encourage serious discussion about the source of our belief. Do we truly base our belief on God's Word or do we base it on man's interpretation of God's Word? The number and variety of religions in our world make it pretty clear that we do not understand or accept God's Word the way he intended. Because we already have a multitude of interpretations of the Bible, I plan to keep my own to a minimum and rely instead on scripture. My hope is to give you as much scripture as I can find on a topic so that you have a basis to form your own opinion. As you know, what is viewed as a sin by one religion may be accepted as healthy behavior by another religion. No wonder we are all so full of guilt and doubt. Filling Christians with guilt to control behavior is a tool used by man. God did not intend it to be that way.

Ephesians 4:4-7, KJV
There is one body, and one spirit, even as ye are called in one hope of your calling; one Lord, one faith, one baptism, one God and father of all, who is above all, and through all, and in

you all. But unto every one of us is given grace according to the measure of the gift of Christ.

The gift of Christ is not a New Testament creation but rather was predicted several times in the Old Testament. Isaiah gives the clearest and most undeniable prediction.

Isaiah 53, NIV

Who has believed our message and to whom has the arm of the Lord been revealed? He grew up before him like a tender shoot, and like a root out of dry ground. He had no beauty or majesty to attract us to him, nothing in his appearance that we should desire him. He was despised and rejected by men, a man of sorrows, and familiar with suffering. Like one from whom men hide their faces he was despised, and we esteemed him not. Surely he took up our infirmities and carried our sorrows, yet we considered him stricken by God, smitten by him, and afflicted. But he was pierced for our transgressions, he was crushed for our iniquities; the punishment that brought us peace was upon him, and by his wounds we are healed. We all, like sheep, have gone astray, each of us has turned to his own way; and the Lord has laid upon him the iniquity of us all. He was oppressed and afflicted, yet he did not open his mouth; he was led like a lamb to the slaughter, and as a sheep before her shearers is silent, so he did not open his mouth. By oppression and judgment he was taken away. And who can speak for his descendants? For he was cut off from the land of the living; for the transgression of my people he was stricken. He was assigned a grave with the wicked and with the rich in his death, though he had done no violence, nor was any deceit in his mouth. Yet it was the Lords will to crush him and cause him to suffer, and though the Lord makes his life a guilt offering, he will see his offspring and prolong his days, and the will of the Lord will prosper in his hand. After the suffering of his soul he will see the light of life and be satisfied; by his knowledge my righteous servant will justify many, and he will bear their iniquities. Therefore I will give him a portion among the great, and he will divide the spoils of the strong, because he poured out his life unto death, and was numbered among the transgressors. For he bore the sins of many and made intercession for the transgressors.

NIV James 1:13–15
When tempted, no one should say, "God is tempting me." For God cannot be tempted by evil, nor does he tempt anyone; but each one is tempted when, by his own evil desire, he is dragged away and enticed. Then, after desire has conceived, it gives birth to sin, and sin, when it is full grown, gives birth to death.

It is very difficult to discuss sin without coming to some understanding of God's relationship with man. There is a character in one of my favorite movies, *Lonesome Dove*, by the name of Woodrow Call. In one memorable scene, Woodrow brutally beats a soldier nearly to death. As the townspeople stare at him in disbelief at his explosion of anger, he explains that he can't abide bad behavior in a man, he won't tolerate it. It's difficult to understand how a loving God can throw someone into a lake of fire, condemning him to an eternity in hell. The best answer I can give you is that God cannot abide sinful behavior in man—he won't tolerate it. How is it possible for him to be a God of love and also be a God of judgment? We seem to have lost our understanding that God is awesome. He is all-powerful. He created the world and everything in it. We have created for ourselves a kinder and gentler God. We would much rather think about God as all-loving instead of omnipotent, fierce, and deadly. God told Moses that it was not possible for him to look at God or Moses would be destroyed. Fear God: you have no authority over him. Trying to control him or put bounds on him is like trying to control a nuclear blast.

Galatians 6:7-8, NIV
Do not be deceived: God cannot be mocked. A man reaps what he sows. The one who sows to please his sinful nature, from that nature will reap destruction; the one who sows to please the Spirit, from the Spirit will reap eternal life.

Romans 9:14-16, NLT
What can we say? Was God being unfair? Of course not! For God said to Moses, "I will show mercy to anyone I choose, and I will show compassion to anyone I choose." So receiving God's promise is not up to us. We can't get it by choosing it or by working hard for it. God will show mercy to anyone he chooses.

Ecclesiastes 12:12-14, KJV
And further, by these, my son, be admonished: of making many books there is no end; and much study is a weariness to the flesh. Let us hear the conclusion of the whole matter Fear God, and keep his commandments: for this is the whole duty of man. For God shall bring every work into judgment, with every secret thing, whether it be good, or whether it be evil.

The awesome thing about our God of limitless power is that he loves mankind and has great compassion for us.

Psalms 51:1-4, NASB

Be gracious to me, O God, according to your loving kindness; According to the greatness of your compassion blot out my transgressions. Wash me thoroughly from my iniquity and cleanse me from my sin. For I know my transgressions, and my sin is ever before me. Against you, you only, I have sinned and done what is evil in your sight, so that you are justified when you speak and blameless when you judge.

God created all of creation, but he was not content until he created man. He created man in his own image so that man could enjoy his companionship. He put Adam and Eve in paradise and kept a very close one on one relationship with them. He gave them one law. One law! Do not eat the fruit from the *tree of knowledge*. When Adam and Eve failed, God removed them from paradise and separated himself from them. God maintained his love for his children and did not give up on them. He loves each one of us completely and did not create us only to destroy us. God gave us the Old Testament covenant and the law to convict us of our sin. He reestablished a more indirect relationship with man through the leaders of his synagogue. Man proved to be unable to keep the law, so man created a multitude of loopholes for himself. Man also created his own laws and passed them off as God's. Some of these laws created by man were made to generate income, some to provide power and control and some as an honest attempt to improve behavior. In the end, as God predicted in his Old Testament books, he sent his son Jesus to be the ultimate sacrifice for the forgiveness of our sins and to establish a new covenant. The new covenant is not based on laws and our works but rather on our belief and faith.

Ephesians 2:8-9, NASB
For by grace you have been saved through faith; and that not of yourselves, it is a gift of God; not as a result of works, that no one should boast.

Along with the new covenant, God also ended his indirect relationship with man-kind. He ended the need to go through church leaders for sacrifice and sin forgiveness and reestablished a one-on-one relationship with us by writing his laws on our hearts and giving us the Holy Spirit.

I know this is an extremely simplified explanation of God's relationship with man and sin. I strongly encourage you to read your own Bibles and come to your own understanding. The bottom line is this. You are literally God's children. He loves you very much. He wants to be with you and have a relationship with you. He cannot tolerate bad behavior and, without question, will pronounce judgment on you. God offers you forgiveness of your sins through the sacrificial blood of his son Jesus.

John 3:16-17, NASB
For God so loved the world that he gave his only begotten son, that whoever believes in him should not perish, but have eternal life. For God did not send the son to judge the world, but that the world should be saved through him.

1 John 2:1-2, NIV
My dear children, J write this to you so that you will not sin. But if anyone does sin, we have one who speaks to the Father in our defense–Jesus Christ, the Righteous One. He is the atoning sacrifice for our sins, and not only for ours but also for the sins of the whole world.

The last thing that I want to emphasize is that there is no human being, now living or who has ever lived, who has not sinned. Yes, I'm talking about Mom and Dad, your grandparents, your minister, your priest, and the pope. You may find that offensive, but I promise you that if you ask any of them directly, they will agree that their lives have not been sin-free.

Romans 3:23, NASB
For all have sinned and fallen short of the glory of God.

1 John 1:8-10, KJV
If we say that we have no sin, we deceive ourselves, and the truth is not in us. If we confess our sins he is faithful and just to forgive us our sins, and to cleanse us from all unrighteousness. If we say that we have not sinned, we make him a liar, and his word is not in us.

You are not exceptional. Your sin is neither worse nor greater than everyone else. To God, sin is sin. Unlike man, who has the need to rate sin to make himself feel better, God's word tells us that the state of sin separates us from him.

James 2:10, NASB
For whoever keeps the whole law and yet stumbles at one point, he has become guilty of all.

Proverbs 6:16–19, NIV
There are six things the Lord hates, seven that are detestable to him: haughty eyes, a lying tongue, hands that shed innocent blood, a heart that devises wicked schemes, feet that are quick to rush to evil, a false witness that pours out lies, and a man who stirs up dissension among brothers.

Whether you cheat on your taxes, tell a few lies, steal, commit adultery, or murder someone, your sin puts you in a state that separates you from God. Do not be afraid to go to church; the church is full of sinners just like you and me. You will find that a body of believers who love God can offer you understanding, love, and support that are difficult to find anywhere else.

Chapter 1

Drinking

Let's start with drinking alcohol. We all know that alcohol has the potential to be addictive, and it has destroyed many families and individuals' lives. Some churches condone drinking and include it in church functions. Other churches condemn drinking in all circumstances and tend to condemn the churches that allow it. One thing is certain: the fact that the word "drunk" appears in the Bible means that drinking in excess occurred both in the Old and New Testaments.

Proverbs 20:1, NIV
Wine is a mocker and beer is a brawler; whoever is led astray by them is not wise.

Other translations say "strong drink" or "liquor" instead of "beer," but in any case, King Solomon's words are just as true now as they were then. Drinking alcohol can affect your life in a negative way. The question is whether God considers it a sin.

Genesis 14:18-20, NASB

And Melchizedek King of Salem brought out bread and wine; now he was a priest of God most high. He blessed him and said, blessed be Abram of God Most High, Possessor of heaven and earth; And blessed be God Most High, Who has delivered your enemies into your hand.

After the destruction of Sodom and Gomorrah, Lot escapes with his two virgin daughters and becomes heavily drunk.

Genesis 19:30-36, NLT

Afterward Lot left Zoar because he was afraid of the people there, and he went to live in a cave in the mountains with his two daughters. One day the older daughter said to her sister, "There isn't a man in this entire area for us to marry, and our father will soon be too old to have children. Come, let's get him drunk with wine, and then we will sleep with him. That way we will preserve our family line through our father. So that night they got him drunk, and the older daughter went in and slept with her father." He was unaware of her lying down or getting up again. The next morning the older daughter said to her younger sister, "I slept with our father last night. Let's get him drunk with wine again tonight, and you go in and sleep with him. That way our family line will be preserved." So that night they got him drunk again, and the younger daughter went in and slept with him. As before he was unaware of her lying down or getting up again. So both of Lots daughters became pregnant by their father.

The Bible simply tells this story as a fact. It does not comment on Lot becoming drunk or on his drunkenness, allowing an incestuous relationship with his daughters to occur.

In Leviticus we find limitations on drinking placed on the Aaronic priesthood.

Leviticus 10:8-9, KJV
And the Lord spake unto Aaron, saying, Do not drink wine or strong drink, thou, nor thy sons with thee, when ye go into the tabernacle of the congregation, lest ye die: it shall be a statute for ever throughout your generations.

Limitations are also placed on leaders of Christian churches. In Paul's first letter to Timothy, we find one of the qualifications for being an overseer, or elder, and for church deacons is not being addicted to wine.

1 Timothy 3:3, NASB
Not addicted to wine or pugnacious, but gentle, peaceable, free from the love of money.

1 Timothy 3:8, NASB
Deacons likewise must be men of dignity, not double tongued, or addicted to too much wine or fond of sordid gain.

Later in Paul's letter to Timothy, we find the following.

1 Timothy 5:23, NIV
Stop drinking only water, and use a little wine because of your stomach and your frequent illnesses.

I should point out that the water quality was pretty poor in Paul's day and often caused health issues.

Ephesians 5:18, NLT
Don't be drunk with wine, because that will ruin your life. Instead, let the Holy Spirit fill and control you.

The first miracle performed by Jesus was turning six twenty to thirty gallon pots of water into wine.

John 2:1-11, NASB
And on the third day there was a wedding in Cana of Galilee, and the mother of Jesus was there; and Jesus was also invited, and his disciples, to the wedding. And when the wine gave out, the mother of Jesus said to him, "They have no wine." And Jesus said to her, "Women, what do I have to do with you? My hour has not yet come." His mother said to the servants, "Whatever he says to you, do it." Now there were six stone waterpots set there for the Jewish custom of purification, containing twenty or thirty gallons each. Jesus said to them, "Fill the waterpots with water." And they filled them to the brim. And he said to them, "Draw some out now and take it to the headwaiter." And they took it to him. And when the headwaiter tasted the water which had become wine, and did not know where it came from (but the servants who had drawn the water knew), the headwaiter called the bridegroom, and said to him, "Every man serves the good wine first, and when men have drunk freely, then that which is poorer; you have kept the good wine until now." This beginning of his signs Jesus did in Cana of Galilee, and manifested his glory, and his disciples believed in him.

I always find it amusing that Jesus didn't want to turn the water to wine, but his mom completely ignored him. We hear very little about Jesus growing up, but it seems pretty obvious that Mom was confident that Jesus could perform this miracle. Jesus used the miracle to gain the belief of his disciples. There is no way that Jesus would have performed this miracle if drinking was a sin. Jewish weddings were not the one-day affairs of today. They lasted several days, but nevertheless, the water was turned into wine after the "wine gave out." When all of the other wine had been consumed, Jesus made about 180 gallons of some very good wine. But while God's Word does not say that man should not drink, it makes it very clear that he should not get drunk.

Ephesians 5:18, KJV
And be not drunk with wine, wherein is excess.

1 Corinthians 5:11, NIV
But now I am writing you that you must not associate with anyone who calls himself a brother but is sexually immoral or greedy, an idolater or a slanderer, a drunkard or a swindler. With such a man do not eat.

Luke 21:34, NLT
Watch out! Don't let me find you living in careless ease and drunkenness and filled with the worries of this life.

Romans 13:13, NLT
We should be decent and true in everything we do, so that everyone can approve of our behavior. Don't participate in wild parties and getting drunk, or in adultery and immoral living, or in fighting and jealousy.

Galatians 5:19–21, NASB
Now the deeds of the flesh are evident, which are: immorality, impurity, sensuality, idolatry, sorcery, enmities, strife, jealousy, outburst of anger, disputes, dissensions, factions, envy-

ing, drunkenness, carousing, and things like these, of which *J* forewarn you, just as *J* have forewarned you, that those who practice such things will not inherit the kingdom of God.

Those who condemn drinking use the following verses to make their point.

Romans 14:20-21, NIV
Do not destroy the work of God for the sake of food. All food is clean, but it is wrong for a man to eat anything that causes someone else to stumble. *Jt* is better not to eat meat or drink wine or to do anything else that will cause your brother to fall.

That is a powerful verse and difficult to debate. Man created this issue for himself. God does not see drinking as a sin. The qualifications he sets for the leaders of his church are that they should not be addicted to much wine. God does see getting drunk as a sin. At some point in time, man determined that drinking was sinful and made a large portion of the world believe it. Now many Christians feel guilty about drinking and avoid drinking in public so they do not cause someone else to stumble. I would like to point out something else in reference to several of the above scriptures. When references are made to refraining from associating with sinners who get drunk, etc., they are talking about Christians not associating with other Christians. They are not talking about avoiding non-Christians.

1 Corinthians 5:9-11, NLT
When J wrote to you before, J told you not to associate with people who indulge in sexual sin. But J wasn't talking about unbelievers who indulge in sexual sin, or who are greedy or are swindlers or idol worshipers. You would have to leave this world to avoid people like that. What J meant was that you are not to associate with anyone who claims to be a Christian yet indulges in sexual sin, or is greedy, or worships idols, or is abusive, or a drunkard, or a swindler. Don't even eat with such people.

That took a while to get to the "drunkard" part, but I couldn't leave the rest out and still make it understandable. Caution must also be used here when talking about not associating with other Christians who are sinners. As we have already discussed, the church is full of sinners, you and me among them. What Paul is talking about is people who claim to be Christians and know right from wrong yet blatantly continue to sin. Allowing that kind of blatant sin to continue within the body of believers makes their sin seem acceptable and therefore is a bad influence on young Christians or others who struggle with the same sin. For those Christians who sin in this way, the outlook is dire. God's judgment is harsh for those who lead people away from him.

Hebrews 10:26-27, NIV
If we deliberately keep on sinning after we have received the knowledge of the truth, no sacrifice for sins is left, but only a fearful expectation of judgment and of raging fire that will consume the enemies of God.

I'll leave you with this last scripture, which came straight from Jesus. He was talking to a crowd about the Pharisees who had rejected John the Baptist's baptism and also rejected Jesus. What he is saying is that it is impossible to make the Pharisees happy.

Luke 7:31-34, NLT
"How shall I describe this generation?" Jesus asked, "With what shall I compare them? They are like a group of children playing a game in the public square. They complain to their friends, "We played wedding songs, and you weren't happy, so we played funeral songs, but you weren't sad." For John the Baptist didn't drink wine and he often fasted, and you say, "He is demon possessed." And I, the Son of Man, feast and drink, and you say, "He's a glutton and a drunkard, and a friend of the worst sort of sinners!"

None of the above scriptures say that drinking alcohol is a sin. The scriptures do say that being drunk or a drunkard is sinful. If drinking takes up the majority of your free time, harms the well-being of your family, has a negative effect on your marriage, or affects your ability or desire to tithe, you are showing your inability to control your need to drink. All of us have temptations that we struggle to control. Satan takes advantage of our weaknesses to destroy our relationship with God and our families and even to use us as Christians to make God and Christianity look bad. Your only choice if you are unable to control it is to abstain completely. Seek help from God and your Church family; it's the only way you will be able to stop satan from using your weakness against you.

Chapter 2

Gambling

There are no verses in the Bible where the word "gambling" appears. There are a few verses where the casting of lots took place.

1 Samuel 14:42-43, NIV
Saul said "Cast the lot between me and Jonathan my son." And Jonathan was taken. Then Saul said to Jonathan, "Tell me what you have done."

The following verse is from Psalms and is a prediction of the Messiah's coming.

Psalms 22:16-18, KJV
For dogs have compassed me: The assembly of the wicked have enclosed me: They pierced my hands and my feet. I may tell all my bones: They look and stare upon me. They part my garments among them, and cast lots upon my vesture.

Jonah 1:7, NLT
Then the crew cast lots to see which one of them had offended the Gods and caused the terrible storm.

John 19:24, NIV
"Let's not tear it," they said to one another, "Let's decide by lot who will get it." This happened that the scripture might be

fulfilled which said, "They divided my garments among them and cast lots for my clothing."

Acts 1:26, NASB
And they drew lots for them, and the lot fell to Matthias; and he was added to the eleven apostles.

That last verse tells of the apostles themselves casting lots for the replacement of Judas. Many people associate casting lots with gambling, but its main function was a form of decision making. In the case of the apostles, they believed that the will of God would be revealed through the casting of lots. As with drinking, gambling can devastate lives and families. God, however, is silent on this issue. Again as with drinking, man decided at some point in time that gambling was a sin creating a great deal of unnecessary guilt. God does not see gambling as a sin. However, being addicted to gambling is sinful because of the addiction. Like drinking, if gambling takes up the majority of your free time, harms the well-being of your family, has a negative effect on your marriage, or affects your ability or desire to tithe, you are showing your inability to control your need to gamble.

Chapter 3

Addictions

The Bible does not directly address addictions of any kind. The closest it comes is with being a drunkard. The word "drunkard" found in the various lists of what God considers sin connotes a loss of control or an addiction. Any form of an addiction, whether to alcohol, food, drugs, sex, pornography, or gambling, is a complete loss of self-control and creates ruin in the individual, his family, and possibly his friends and fellow Christians. An addiction becomes idolatry when it becomes the most important thing in your life.

1 Corinthians 3:16-17, NASB
Do you not know that you are a temple of God and that the Spirit of God dwells in you? If any man destroys the temple of God, God will destroy him, for the temple of God is Holy, and that is what you are.

The New Living Translation (NLT) states verse 16 a little differently.

1 Corinthians 3:16, NLT
Don't you realize that all of you together are the temple of God and that the Spirit of God lives in you?

That may sound like a very big difference, but in God's eyes, all members of the church become one body. While each person maintains his own individuality, he also becomes a functioning part of the church body. The gift that God has blessed you with is used by the body to make it whole. Whether you are the voice, the heart, the brain, or the hand, you are one working part of the whole body. No matter how insignificant your part may seem, you have the power to influence the entire body. The final word on this topic is also found in Corinthians.

1 Corinthians 6:12, NLT
You may say, "I am allowed to do anything." But I reply, "Not everything is good for you." And even though "I am allowed to do anything, I must not become a slave to anything."

You may say, "But God made me this way." That may or may not be true, but God is the only one who can give you the strength to change the way you are. You cannot conquer your addiction on your own. Turn it over to God with much prayer, and he will give you the strength to resist. When you have turned it over to God, you must also learn to use him to shut down your fantasies as soon as they begin. Fantasies have tremendous power. They tend to start out harmless, but if you allow yourself to indulge in them, they begin to trigger physical reactions, pumping your body's own pleasure drugs into your system. Achieving a full-blown fantasy with your body quivering in excitement and anticipation takes you to a point of no return. You may be able to enjoy the rush and resist for a while, but it is only a matter of time before you give yourself over to it. Ask God to stop that process as soon as you realize it is beginning, and he will. If you are struggling with an addiction, you can never indulge in those fantasies again. Please do not misconstrue what I am saying. I am not saying that all fantasy is bad. What I am saying is that satan uses fantasy as a powerful tool to exploit our weaknesses. Do not try to fight this battle with satan by yourself. Only through Scripture, prayer, fellowship and support of other Christians, and the assurance of God's love will you be able to fight that fight.

2 Corinthians 12:7-10, NASB

And because of the surpassing greatness of the revelations, for this reason, to keep me from exalting myself, there was given me a thorn in the flesh, a messenger of satan to buffet me-to keep me from exalting myself! Concerning this I entreated the Lord three times that it might depart from me. And he has said to me, "My grace is sufficient for you, for power is perfected in weakness." Most gladly therefore, I will rather boast about my weakness, that the power of Christ may dwell in me. Therefore I am well content with weaknesses, with insults, with distresses, with persecutions, with difficulties, for Christ sake; for when I am weak, then I am strong.

God did not take Paul's thorn in the flesh away from him, but God did give him the strength he needed to live with it. God loves you very much, and he will do the same thing for you.

Chapter 4

Food

The topic of food is sure to be controversial. It was very controversial during the time of Jesus also. As with many other religions, Jews had many restrictions on the foods they were allowed to eat. When God gave man the new covenant, he was no longer only the God of the Jews but made himself accessible to the rest of mankind.

Romans 9:25-26, HCSB
As he says in Hosea: I will call "Not-My-People," "My-People," and she who is "Unloved," "Beloved." And it will be in the place where they were told, you are not my people, there they will be called sons of the living God.

The foods that were unclean were eaten freely by most other races, the "Gentiles," and were a major source of conflict for the Jews. In addition to a restrictive list of unclean foods, the Jews were not allowed to eat any food that had been sacrificed to other gods or idols. The new covenant was given to man because the law had become so abused by the Pharisees that it was a burden to God's followers. The new covenant changed our salvation from one earned by following the letter of the law to one established by God's grace.

Ephesians 2:8-9, NIV
For it is by grace you have been saved, through faith—and this not of yourselves, it is the gift of God—not by works, so that no one can boast.

The grace of God became available to man when Jesus became the final sacrificial Lamb of God and took the sins of mankind upon him, erasing them from the sight of God. Because of the sinfulness of man, it is impossible for anyone to be good enough to earn his own way into heaven. Even today when God willingly offers us his grace, we continue to try to earn it on our own. One of the ways that we try to earn our own salvation is by creating rules to follow. If we don't cuss, dance, drink, gamble, or eat the wrong food on the wrong day, we think we can become good enough to please God, earning our way to salvation.

1 Corinthians 8:8, HCSB
Food will not make us acceptable to God. We are not inferior if we don't eat, and we are not better if we do eat.

Colossians 2:16, NLT
So don't let anyone condemn you for what you eat or drink, or for not celebrating certain holy days or New Moon ceremonies or Sabbaths.

Colossians 2:20-23, NLT
You have died with Christ, and he has set you free from the evil powers of this world. So why do you keep on following

rules of the world, such as, "Don't handle, don't eat, don't touch?" Such rules are mere human teaching about things that are gone as soon as we use them. These rules may seem wise because they require strong devotion, humility, and severe bodily discipline. But they have no effect when it comes to conquering a person's evil thoughts or desires.

1 Timothy 4:1-5, NIV
The Spirit clearly says that in the latter times some will abandon the faith and follow deceiving spirits and things taught by demons. Such teachings come through hypocritical liars, whose consciences have been seared as with a hot iron. They forbid people to marry and order them to abstain from certain foods, which God created to be received with thanksgiving by those who believe and who know the truth. For everything God created is good, and nothing is to be rejected if it is received with thanksgiving. Because it is consecrated by the word of God and by prayer.

Hebrews 13:9, HCSB
Don't be led astray by various kinds of strange teachings; for it is good for the heart to be established by grace and not by foods, since those involved in them have not benefited.

1 Corinthians 10:23, NLT
You say, "I am allowed to do anything" – but not everything is helpful. You say, "I am allowed to do anything" – but not everything is beneficial. Don't think only of your own good. Think of other Christians and what is best for them.

1 Corinthians 29-32, NLT
Now why should my freedom be limited by what someone else thinks? If I can thank God for the food and enjoy it, why should I be condemned for eating it? Whatever you eat or drink or whatever you do, you must do all for the glory of

God. Don't give offense to Jews or Gentiles or the church of God.

1 Cor. 9:27

Finally, we should mention why Friday abstinence was imposed. The Church recognizes that, since meat is a chief part of most meals served in most places, and since meat is usually the most valued or expensive part of a meal, abstinence from meat on Fridays is a good way for Christians to unite themselves more closely to the sufferings of their Lord (Rom. 8:16–17, 1 Pet. 2:21) by denying themselves something they enjoy. Abstinence from meat is a sacrifice which unites them in penance and strengthens the solidarity of the Church through mild suffering. It's also a good form of mortification, which disciplines the soul and strengthens its resistance to concupiscence. Paul practiced and recommended mortification: "I drive my body and train it, for fear that after having preached to others, I myself should be disqualified".

The above quote was taken from the Catholic Answers website. As you can see, the intent is good. Fasting is recommended throughout the Bible. Denying yourself in an effort to bring you closer to God is a good thing. It is a self-test that keeps you aware that God is more important than anything else in your life. It becomes a problem when a failure to fast or participate in abstinence becomes viewed as a sin. I suppose it is the sinful nature of man that gives him the ability to take anything intended for good and make it something bad. I had to look up the word "concupiscence." The *Oxford Universal Dictionary* defines it as "vehement desire; in Theol. Use, desire for the things of the world. Libidinous desire, sexual appetite, lust." Of course they have to use a word no one knows to describe a word no one knows. "Libidinous" is defined as "given to, full of, or characterized by lust; lustful lecherous, lewd." I think we get the idea. I may as well define "mortification" while I'm at it. Mortification means, in religious use: "The action of mortifying the flesh or its lust by the practice of austere living, esp. by the self-infliction of bodily pain or discomfort." Some religious individuals take mortification to extremes by having themselves nailed to a cross, wrapping barbed wire around their legs, or whipping themselves until they bleed. I will flatly say that there is no biblical precedent for self-mutilation. God's Word does not say that we must suffer if we are followers of Christ. It says that we probably will suffer for being his followers. There is precedent for self-denial, fasting, and extended hours of prayer. The point is this: if food, or any other addictive item for that matter, has become so important to you that you can't do without it for one day, you probably have a problem. In reality, the Catholic Church is being very lenient in asking its followers to abstain from only warm-blooded meat one day a week. Training yourself to resist meat for a day serves to strengthen your ability to resist other strong temptations. The bottom line is that it is a good practice, but it is not a sin if you choose not to do it.

The last thing to cover here is food addiction that leads to obesity. Food addiction has to be one of the toughest things in the world to gain control of. Almost all other addictions can be eliminated completely, as hard as that is, and life goes on. You can't stop eating. Losing weight makes you look and feel better, but all of those fat cells are still there screaming to be refilled. There is a sad but hard fact, though, when it comes to addictions and God. If food has become an idol to you and having it is more important to you than God, it is a sin. I know that is a tough stance to take.

You may ask yourself, "Why does the New Testament scriptures say it is all right to eat anything when the Old Testament scriptures clearly state that many foods were unclean, such as pork, and that eating unclean foods was a sin? The scriptures saying what not to eat are numerous, and I don't want to list them all. Read chapter 11 of Leviticus for an extensive list. The gist is that you could not eat any animal that did not "both" chew its cud and have split hooves. For example, a rabbit chews its cud but does not have split hooves, while a pig has split hooves but does not chew its cud. You could not eat any animal that walked on paws. You could not eat anything out of the water that did not have scales or fins. You could not eat birds of prey. You could not eat moles, mice, lizards, or reptiles. You could not eat flying insects that did not hop. Why God gave those restrictions to the Jews, his chosen people, is beyond my understanding. What I do understand is that when God sent his Son, he no longer restricted himself to the Jews but offered himself to all of mankind. With the death of

Jesus, a new covenant was established based on faith and God's grace bringing an end to the impossibility of earning your own righteousness by following the letter of the law. Does that mean that the law has been abolished? In Matthew 5:17, Jesus himself said, "Do not think that I came to abolish the Law of the Prophets'; I did not come to abolish, but to fulfil." His sacrificial blood covered the sins of all who believe in him. He fulfilled the law by becoming the Lamb of God, bringing an end to the need for regular sin sacrifice. In the same way, the New Covenant brought by Jesus ended restrictions on food when God became the God of all. God made it clear in Acts 10 when he sent Peter a vision.

Acts 10:11-16, NASB

And he saw the sky opened up, and an object like a great sheet coming down, lowered by four corners to the ground, and there were in it all kinds of four-footed animals and crawling creatures of the earth and birds of the air. A voice came to him, "Get up, Peter, kill and eat!" But Peter said, "By no means, Lord, for I have never eaten anything unholy and unclean." Again a voice came to him a second time, "What God has cleansed, no longer consider unholy." This happened three times, and immediately the object was taken into the sky.

This is a long story, so I recommend that you read all of chapter 10 and the first part of chapter 11 of Acts. To keep it short, at the same time Peter had his vision, God was working in the life of an uncircumcised Gentile named Cornelius, a God-fearing man, and gave him a vision to send for Peter. Peter went to this Gentile household and gave them the good news about Jesus. When Peter witnessed the Holy Spirit descend upon the entire household and saw them speaking in tongues and exalting God, he understood the meaning of his vision.

Acts 10:34–35, NASB

Opening his mouth, Peter said: "I most certainly understand now that God is not one to show partiality, but in every nation the man who fears him and does what is right is welcome to him.

Peter baptized the entire household and stayed long enough to eat food he had previously been forbidden to eat with them.

Chapter 5

Idols

For most Americans, the idea of worshiping an idol is only a concept that we read about in the Bible or history books. There are still many places in today's world though where idol worship is alive and well. Idol worship also takes place when we become addicted to something and our addiction becomes the focus of our life instead of God. Addicts do not exactly bow down and pray to or worship their addiction, but it consumes them with desire. The addiction becomes more important than God, family, friends, or even their own life. In that sense, your idol becomes the thing that you desire most in your life. Idols described in the Bible are creations of God such as the sun or moon, things created by man's hand such as golden calves, or other gods, such as Thor or Odin. These idols are used as true items of worship and whole religions are based on the prayer, worship, and even sacrifices offered to them. The first of the Ten Commandments makes it very clear where God stands on this issue.

Exodus 20:2-6, KJV
I am the Lord thy God, which have brought thee out of the land of Egypt, out of the house of bondage. Thou shalt have no other Gods before me. Thou shalt not make unto thee any graven image, or likeness of any thing that is in Heaven above, or that is in the Earth beneath, or that is in the water under the Earth: Thou shalt not bow down thyself to them, nor serve them: for I the Lord thy God am a jealous God, visiting the iniquity of the fathers upon the children unto the third and fourth generation of them that hate me; and showing mercy unto thousands of them that love me, and keep my commandments.

Leviticus 19:4, NASB
Do not turn to idols or make for yourself molten Gods; I am the Lord your God.

Deuteronomy 27:15, KJV
Cursed be the man that maketh any graven or molten image, an abomination unto the Lord, the work of the hands of the craftsman, and putteth it in a secret place.

Psalm 95:8-11, HCSB
Do not harden your hearts as at Meribah, as on that day at Massah in the wilderness where your fathers tested me; they tried me, though they had seen what I did. For forty years I was disgusted with that generation; I said, "They are a people whose hearts go astray; they do not know my ways." So I swore in my anger, "They will not enter my rest."

An entire generation of Jews were not allowed to enter the Promised Land and perished in the desert during that forty-year journey because they did not understand the nature of God. Idol worship is a serious sin and will not be tolerated by God. If you are kneeling before or bowing down to or praying to anything other than God, you should stop. There is no human being, statue, jewelry, icon, image, or creation of God or man that God deems as acceptable to be worshipped. Peter, Paul, and John all told men who had fallen down to worship them to stop and get up because they were only human.

Acts 10:25-26, NASB

When Peter entered, Cornelius met him, and fell at his feet and worshipped him. But Peter raised him up saying, "Stand up; I too am just a man."

The apostle John himself fell at the feet of an angel to worship him, but was told to stop.

Revelation 22:8-9, NIV

I, John, am the one who saw and heard all these things, and when I saw and heard these things, I fell down to worship at the feet of the Angel who had been showing them to me. But he said to me, "Do not do it! I am a fellow servant with you and your brothers the prophets, and of all who keep the words of this book. Worship God!"

If Peter did not view himself to be worthy of worship and an angel of God is not worthy to be worshiped, then no human, now living or who has ever lived, is worthy. Showing respect and honor is one thing, but kneeling before, bowing to, or praying to anything other than God and his Son is a sin.

Chapter 6

Abortion

We all know the commandment that states, "Thou shalt not kill." What seems to be a simple and clear statement is riddled with contradiction. God himself has taken a multitude of human life. He killed a man for touching the ark. He struck down a husband and wife for lying about a financial sacrifice. He wiped out most of the known world with a flood. We are his creation, and he is a God of judgment, omnipotent, and all-powerful, and one day he will direct that judgment on us. God has also directed his people to kill other men in warfare, even helping them to that end. As Christians, most of us feel that killing in warfare or to protect ourselves and our family is justifiable. On the other hand, Christians and non-Christians alike agree that the taking of an innocent life, or murder, is not justifiable. One argument made in support of abortion is that life does not begin until birth when a child can breathe his first breath and sustain his own life. The Bible does not mention abortion. The Bible does have several scriptures that state that creation takes place in the womb and that God involves himself in that creation.

Psalm 139: 13-16, HCSB
For it was you who created my inward parts; you knit me together in my mother's womb. I will praise you because I have been remarkably and wonderfully made. Your works are wonderful, and I know this very well. My bones were not hidden from you when I was made in secret, when I was formed in the depths of the earth. Your eyes saw me when I was formless; all my days were written in your book and planned before a single one of them began.

Isaiah 44:24, NASB
Thus says the Lord, your redeemer, and the one who formed you from the womb' "I, the Lord, am the maker of all things, stretching out the heavens by myself, and spreading out the earth all alone."

Isaiah 49:1, NLT
Listen to me, all of you in far off lands! The Lord called me before my birth; from within the womb he called me by name.

Isaiah 49:5, KJV
And now, saith the Lord that formed me from the womb to be his servant.

Jeremiah 1:4-5, KJV
Then the word of the Lord came unto me saying, before I formed thee in the belly I knew thee; and before thou camest forth out of the womb I sanctified thee, and I ordained thee a prophet unto the nations.

We are so good at rationalizing that we are able to justify, in our own mind, any of our actions. There is much scientific physical evidence that life in the womb is filled with awareness well before birth. A baby knows its surroundings and the sounds of its mother's voice. It reacts to music, it feels its own hands and feet, and it sucks on its toes and fingers. A beating heart or body movement is not possible without a well-formed and functioning brain. Many babies have been born early in the third trimester and have survived to live normal lives. Some babies have survived birth as early as twenty-four weeks. They are born with viable functioning brains but need help while they wait for organ development, especially lungs and liver. Is our first breath of air the moment when life begins? The bottom line is that it doesn't matter what we think; what matters is what God thinks. I know that rape and incest are terrible things. I know that a child's life must sometimes be taken to save his mother's life. I know that babies are sometimes so deformed in the womb that they can't possibly survive. I do not know if God allows for those things. His Word does not give any indication that he does or does not. The only thing he states is that he is involved in the creation of each life. The truth is that the vast majority of the abortions that occur are the direct result of irresponsible behavior on our own part. Compounding such irresponsible behavior as casual sex, premarital sex, and sex during an adulteress relationship by taking our own child's life cannot possibly be acceptable to God.

If you have already had an abortion, it can be a devastating thing to dwell on. You must accept that you can be forgiven by God. We are all sinners and can only get forgiveness by confessing to God, repenting, and accepting his grace. God does not view your sinful act as any less forgivable than any of mine. God has an extreme love for you and promises his forgiveness.

If you are contemplating an abortion, don't do it. Saving yourself embarrassment or removing an inconvenient burden is not worth it. God may have an adoptive family already in place to love your child. If you decide to keep your child, God will help you, if you let him. Seek him out through scripture and prayer. Seek out help and support through his followers. The consequences of getting pregnant seem unspeakable, but they will pass. Living with the memory of your aborted child takes more than time to heal.

Chapter 7

Premarital Sex

I chose to put this chapter after the chapter on abortion because the main reason for abortions in our society is intercourse outside of marriage. You will not find the term "premarital sex" in the Bible. The term used during the time that the Bible was written is "fornication." The *Oxford Universal Dictionary* defines "fornication" as "voluntary sexual intercourse between a man (strictly an unmarried man) and an unmarried woman." The word is used in many verses throughout the Bible, and I have listed quite a few; however, my list is not exhaustive. It is also worth noting that the Bible does not contain any specific ceremony or method for a couple to become married in God's eyes. God views the act of intercourse as the bond that joins a man to a woman for life.

Genesis 2:24, KJV
Therefore shall a man leave his father and mother, and shall cleave unto his wife: and they shall become one flesh.

Matthew 19:4-6, NIV

"Haven't you read," he replied, "that at the beginning the Creator made them male and female, and said, ' For this reason a man will leave his father and mother and be united to his wife, and the two will become one flesh"? So they are no longer two but one. Therefore what God has joined together let no man separate.

1 Corinthians 6:15-16, NASB

Do you not know that your bodies are members of Christ? Shall I then take away the members of Christ and make them members of a prostitute? May it never be! Or do you not know that the one who joins himself to a prostitute is one body with her? For he says, "The two shall become one flesh."

God sets sexual sin apart from other sins.

1 Corinthians 6:18-20, NIV

Flee from sexual immorality. All other sins a man commits are outside his body, but he who sins sexually sins against his own body. Do you not know that your body is the temple of the Holy Spirit, who is in you whom you have received from God? You are not your own; you were bought for a price. Therefore honor God with your body.

1 Corinthians 7:8-9, NLT

Now I say to those who aren't married and to widows – it's better to stay unmarried, just as I am. But if they can't control themselves, they should go ahead and marry. It is better to marry than to burn with lust.

1 Corinthians 7:1-6, NLT

Now about the questions you asked about in your letter. Yes, it is good to live a celibate life. But because there is so much sexual immorality, each man should have his own wife, and each woman should have her own husband. The husband should not deprive his wife of sexual intimacy, which is her right as a married woman, nor should the wife deprive her husband. The wife gives authority over her body to her husband, and the husband gives authority over his body to his wife. So do not deprive each other of sexual relations. The only exception to this rule would be the agreement of both husband and wife to refrain from sexual intimacy for a limited time, so they can give themselves more completely to prayer. Afterward they should come together again so that satan won't be able to tempt them because of their lack of self-control. This is only my suggestion. It's not meant to be an absolute rule.

Paul makes it pretty clear that the only place a sexual relationship should take place is within a marriage. His urge for Christ's followers to remain single is so they can serve God with all of their being, without their devotion being divided between God and a spouse and children. Some religions have taken this verse as a command for those who serve God not to marry, but that is not the case. If your sexual desires cannot be controlled, it is better to marry.

The following verses all contain references to fornication, as defined as engaging in sexual intercourse while unmarried.

1 Corinthians 6:9, NASB
Or do you not know that the unrighteous will not inherit the kingdom of God? Do not be deceived; neither fornicators, nor idolaters, nor adulterers . . . will inherit the kingdom of God.

Acts 15:28-29, KJV
For it seemed good to the Holy Ghost, and to us, to lay upon you no greater burden than these necessary things; that ye

abstain from meats offered to idols, and from blood, and from things strangled, and from fornication: from which if ye keep yourselves, ye shall do well.

Galatians 5:19-21, KJV
Now the works of the flesh are manifest, which are these; adultery, fornication, uncleanness, lasciviousness . . . of which I tell you before, as I have told you in the past, that they which do such things shall not inherit the kingdom of God.

As you can see, I chose to leave out the sins listed in these verses that are not related to sexual sins. Other translations use words like "sexual immorality," "impurity," "debauchery," "sensuality," and "eagerness for lustful pleasure."

Ephesians 5:3-5, KJV
But fornication, and all uncleanness, or covetousness, let it not be once named amongst you as becometh saints . . . For this ye know, that no whoremonger, nor unclean person, nor covetous who is an idolater, hath any inheritance in the kingdom of Christ and God.

1 Thessalonians 4:3-5, KJV
For this is the will of God, even your sanctification that ye should abstain from fornication: that every one of you should know how to possess his vessel in sanctification and honour; not in the lust of concupiscence, even as the Gentiles which know not God.

Again the other translations use "sexual immorality," and instead of "concupiscence," they use "lustful passion." The hard thing here is that God created us with a natural desire for the opposite sex. He intended sex to be used not only for reproduction but also as a means to bond a relationship and to express love and affection. A passionate sexual relationship within a marriage has God's blessing. A sexual relationship outside of marriage does not have that blessing and is a sin. We have lost control of our children when it comes to relationships with the opposite sex. In many other countries and even in our own history, the chastity of young girls has been carefully guarded. Girls and boys were not allowed to be together without supervision until marriage. Of course, the burden of this protection fell on the girls, depriving them of the freedom they now enjoy through women's liberation. Somehow we have to educate our children that with freedom comes great responsibility. Our government, our society, and our school systems cannot be expected to teach our children to respect and honor each other enough to wait for marriage. The only hope for improvement is for Christian families and churches to work together to teach their children about the wonders of sex and the way God intends them to enjoy it. The idea of churches and Christian families teaching sex to their children may seem hard to accept, but we can clearly see the result of our reluctance to do so. If you are not married, put off having intercourse. Do not be blinded by lust before you truly get to know the person you are with. In the eyes of God, "the two become one flesh" once you engage in sexual intercourse. We have come to see premarital sex as part of our journey in getting to know each other and a help in determining our compatibility. The sad result of this view of sex is that it contributes to our high divorce rate. The trouble with establishing a sexual relationship early in the dating process is that we fall in lust with each other, which is very hard to distinguish from love until the lust wears off. A lustful relationship is a selfish one driven by the desire to fulfill your own needs. Love on the other hand is a selfless relationship where your lover's needs are more important than your own.

Chapter 8

Adultery

It is a natural progression for this chapter to follow the previous chapter on premarital sex. There is no question in anyone's mind, Christian or not, that adultery is sinful. After all, it is listed as one of the Ten Commandments. Even for non-Christians, an adulterous relationship is a marriage killer and not commonly seen as acceptable behavior. As I mentioned in the previous chapter, in our own past and in other cultures, a woman's chastity was held in high regard. By removing sex as an option during dating, couples were forced to get to know each other and find other reasons for enjoying each other's company. While discord happens between the best of friends, the likelihood of a relationship based on friendship staying intact is greater than one based on lust. When we are able to marry our best friend, the act of sex deepens and fulfills that relationship as God intended. It is important to note that God not only intends sex to deepen and fulfill a marriage, but he instructs us to understand that it is a responsibility that couples have to each other.

1 Corinthians 7:1-6, NIV

Now for the matters you wrote about: it is good for a man not to marry. But since there is so much immorality, each man should have his own wife, and each woman her own husband. The husband should fulfill his marital duty to his wife, and likewise the wife to her husband. The wife's body does not belong to her alone but also to her husband. In the same way, the husband's body does not belong to him alone but also to his wife. Do not deprive each other except by mutual consent and for a time, so that you may devote yourselves to prayer. Then come together again so that satan will not tempt you because of your lack of self-control. I say this as a concession, not as a command.

I used a different translation than in the previous chapter, but I had to reuse this scripture. So much is being said here that it is hard to know where to begin. Because we are self-centered by nature, the likelihood of abuse of this scripture is high. You are not being given permission to rape your spouse or force yourself on your spouse against his or her will. I must emphasize the part where it says your body is not "yours alone" but also your spouse's. This scripture is talking about consensual sex. By all means, your body is "yours" to give or not to give, but it is not "yours alone." Scripture however does not pull any punches. Sex is only to be withheld for very good reasons. Two of those reasons mentioned in scripture are devotion to prayer, as noted above, and to abstain from sex during the woman's period, as noted in Leviticus.

Leviticus 20:18, HCSB
If a man sleeps with a menstruating woman and has sexual intercourse with her, he has exposed the source of her flow and she has uncovered the source of her blood. Both of them must be cut off from their people.

That is not to say that there are not more good reasons for withholding sex, just that there aren't many. Sex is not only for sharing love and affection but also for helping your spouse fight lustful urges and a lack of self-control. God does not refer to it as a passionate whim but a marital duty. Some have argued that the only purpose for sex is reproduction and it should end after its purpose has been served, but that is clearly not God's intention.

Exodus 20:14, KJV
Thou shalt not commit adultery.

Deuteronomy 5:18, NASB
You shall not commit adultery.

Galatians 5:19, NLT
When you follow the desires of your sinful nature, your lives will produce these evil results: sexual immorality, impure thoughts, eagerness for lustful pleasure.

King James says "adultery, fornication, uncleanness, lasciviousness."

Hebrews 13:4, NASB
Marriage is to be held in honor among all, and the marriage bed is to be undefiled; for fornicators and adulterers God will judge.

The final verse that I will quote is very hard for us to accept. It comes straight from the mouth of Jesus. It has taken many years for me to finally understand.

Matthew 5:27-28, NLT
You have heard that the law of Moses says, "Do not commit adultery." But I say, anyone who even looks at a women with lust in his eye has already committed adultery with her in his heart.

A verse out of James that was quoted at the beginning of this book helps to explain why Jesus said that.

James 1:13-15, NASB
Let no one say when he is tempted, "I am being tempted by God", for God cannot be tempted by evil, and he himself does not tempt anyone. But each one is tempted when he is carried away and enticed by his own lust. Then when lust has conceived, it gives birth to sin; and when sin is accomplished, it brings forth death.

When you are mentally undressing someone with your eyes and beginning to think what it might be like to be with them, you are beginning to be carried away by your own lust and desire. You may not even think you would ever act on the thought, but a tiny seed of lust has been conceived in your heart. Jesus is saying to nip those thoughts in the bud, and they won't give birth to sin.

Chapter 9

Divorce

The world says that there are two main causes of divorce: sex and money. I maintain that there is only one main cause of divorce, and that is selfishness. Either a spouse was never truly in love or they have been disillusioned to the point where they have fallen out of love and no longer see their spouse as more important than themselves. It quickly becomes an unbearable situation when one or both parties in a marriage become selfish. It may seem like an oversimplification, but I believe that every issue that leads to divorce stems from self-centeredness. Every natural instinct that we have for survival makes our own welfare the most important thing to us. Only by putting God first in our lives are we truly able bring that self-survival instinct under control. I will openly admit that having God first in my life has saved my marriage. Several times in my forty-five years of marriage I have been unhappy enough to end it. I know that my wife has been in the same position. A reluctance to pay child support and the thought of losing a close relationship with my children helped deter me, but the biggest reason I stayed in my marriage was that I could not see a future for myself in which I would not be committing adultery in God's eyes. What my wife and I found was that we had no alternative but to work things out. The amazing thing was that over time, we fell back in love with each other. I'm sorry to say that this happened on more than one occasion in our marriage, but we are still together and currently in love thanks to God being first in our lives. There is nothing that serves satan better than the destruction of families. Dividing families up and scattering them around, taking away stability, distancing them from God, and filling them with guilt serves him well. He does it by festering selfish desires within us and making those tiny seeds of our own lust available at a moment's notice. Every time my wife and I fell out of love in our relationship, it was because we felt that our spouse was being selfish and that our needs were not being met. We became blind to the fact that a person who can only focus on his or her own wants and desires is the one who is being selfish.

Here are some simple solutions to reducing divorce in our world. Put God first in your life. Raise your children with the same belief. Place a high value on your children's chastity. Make it as difficult as possible for them to have opportunities for sexual encounters. I know you may say, "Duh," but in reality, we don't take it seriously. We are much too reluctant to restrict our children's freedom. Preach, preach, and preach some more the need to become friends with each other before sex. Once sex enters into a relationship, everything changes. Falling in lust with each other tends to make us blind. Understand that in God's eyes, sexual inter-course binds two people together inseparably. "The two become one flesh." God intended sex to be given in love. In love, sex is a self-less act and a wonderful and beautiful thing. In lust, it is a selfish act with the beauty reduced to addictive pleasure. Marriage means that your body is no longer only your own but also belongs to your spouse. God did not intend for sex to be for the production of offspring only. He intentionally made it an act of pleasure to bind couples together. He also intended it to be used by couples to protect their spouses from satan because of their lack of self-control. Understand that what God has joined together, he does not want separated. Getting to really know your partner before you commit is pretty serious. It is a lifelong commitment. Selfishness is the breaker of relationships. If your partner is selfish while you're dating, you should probably rethink a lifelong commitment.

Matthew 19:9, NIV
I tell you that anyone who divorces his wife, except for marital unfaithfulness, and marries another woman commits adultery.

Matthew 19:3-8, NLT
Some Pharisees came and tried to trap him with this question: "Should a man be allowed to divorce his wife for any reason?" Haven't you read, he replied, that at the beginning the Creator made them male and female, and said "For this

reason a man will leave his father and mother and be united to his wife, and the two will become one flesh?" So they are no longer two, but one. Therefore what God has joined together, let man not separate. Why then, they asked, did Moses command that a man give his wife a certificate of divorce and send her away? Jesus replied, Moses permitted you to divorce your wives because your hearts were hard. But it was not this way from the beginning.

1 Corinthians 7:10–11, HCSB
I command the married-not I, but the Lord-a wife is not to leave her husband. But if she does leave, she must remain unmarried or be reconciled to her husband-and a husband is not to leave his wife.

1 Corinthians 7:27, NASB
Are you bound to a wife? Do not seek to be released.

1 Corinthians 7:39, NIV
A woman is bound to her husband as long as he lives. But if her husband dies, she is free to marry anyone she wishes, but he must belong to the lord.

Malachi 2:16, NASB
For I hate divorce, says the Lord, the God of Israel.

Mark 10:10–12, KJV
And in the house his disciples asked him again of the same matter. And he saith unto them, whosoever shall put away his wife, and marry another, committeth adultery against her. And if a woman shall put away her husband, and be married to another, she committeth adultery.

Matthew 5:31–33, NIV
"It has been said, Anyone who divorces his wife must give her a certificate of divorce". But I tell you that anyone who

divorces his wife, except for marital unfaithfulness, causes her to become an adulteress, and anyone who marries the divorced woman commits adultery.

I believe that these verses are painfully clear. I hope you can see why my wife and I decided it was better to remain married and to work out our differences. I know this is going to be very difficult for many people because of the high rate of divorce in our country. For those of you who are already divorced and remarried, you cannot change the past. You can, however, ask for forgiveness from a God who loves you more than your own parents. God hates all sin, not just this one. He sent his Son as a living sacrifice for our sins, and through Christ's blood, he no longer sees them. We are directed to confess our sins to God, ask for forgiveness, and then to go and sin no more. If you choose to do that, you must then accept God's forgiveness; it is very real.

To answer the question of whether it is a sin to get a divorce, from my understanding of scripture, the answer is no; it is not a sin. Engaging in a sexual relationship with someone else or remarrying after a divorce, unless your divorce resulted from the infidelity of your spouse, however, is committing adultery and is a sin. Personally, I did not feel that I could live a celibate single life if I were to divorce, so I was forced to reconcile my differences with my spouse and remain in my marriage. The lesson that I hope you learn from my experience is that my wife and I fell back in love with each other.

Scripture also says that marrying a person who was divorced for any other reason than the marital infidelity of their spouse is committing adultery. As unfair as it seems, if you are in an abusive relationship which results in a divorce, you should not remarry but remain single. I am not speaking for God, but my opinion is that you should not remain in a physically or mentally abusive relationship.

Chapter 10

Homosexuality

Because of the extremely controversial nature of this topic, I feel the need to approach it differently than I have the rest of this book. I believe that many people will skip the rest of the book and turn directly to this chapter. Because I expect that to happen, I will try to make this chapter able to stand on its own. What that means is that you may find several statements and scriptures that have appeared previously in the book. My goal is the same, which is to let scripture speak, but this chapter will be much more extensive and contain more scripture.

Our tendency is to deny our own sin and talk about the sins of others or maintain that our own sin is minor compared to the sin of others. To God, sin is sin. There is no difference in God's eyes in the seriousness of gossip, slander, and lying than the seriousness of stealing, adultery, and murder. No human being who has ever lived or is living today is without sin.

Romans 3:23, KJV
For all have sinned and come short of the glory of God.

1 John 1:8, NLT
If we say we have no sin, we are only fooling ourselves and refusing to accept the truth.

1 John 1:10, NLT
If we claim we have not sinned, we are calling God a liar and showing that his word has no place in our hearts.

Our next line of defense is to say "God made me this way," thereby shifting any blame away from ourselves and putting it back on God.

James 1:13–15, NASB
Let no one say when he is tempted, "I am being tempted by God", for God cannot be tempted by evil, and he himself does not tempt anyone. But each one is tempted when he is carried away and enticed by his own lust. Then when lust has conceived, it gives birth to sin; and when sin is accomplished, it brings forth death.

Romans 3:10–18, NLT
As the scriptures say, "No one is good-not even one. No one has real understanding; no one is seeking God. All have turned away from God; all have gone wrong. No one does good, not even one. Their talk is foul, like the stench from an open grave. Their speech is filled with lies. The poison of a deadly snake drips from their lips. Their mouths are full of cursing and bitterness. They are quick to commit murder. Wherever they go, destruction and misery follow them. They do not know what true peace is. They have no fear of God to restrain them."

We haven't learned much after all this time because we are still living with little fear of God to restrain us. We prefer to live our lives in heavenly bliss, seeing God solely as our Father in heaven who is all-forgiving and overflowing with love for us. That view of God is completely true. There is no earthly being, including parents, spouses, or even our children, who has more love and concern for us than God. The problem is that it is only a half-truth, and we choose to ignore the other half. God is a God of judgment. If we choose to reject him and rebel against him, God will most assuredly pass a terrible judgment against us.

Ecclesiastes 12:13-14, KJV
Let us hear the conclusion of the whole matter: Fear God, and keep his commandments: for this is the whole duty of man. For God shall bring every work into judgment, with every secret thing, whether it be good, or whether it be evil.

Psalm 5:4-6, HCSB
For you are not a God who delights in wickedness; evil cannot lodge with you. The boastful cannot stand in your presence; you hate evil doers. You destroy those who tell lies; the Lord abhors a man of bloodshed and treachery.

1 Samuel 2:10, NIV
Those who contend with the Lord will be shattered; against them he will thunder in the heavens, The Lord will judge the ends of the earth.

Mathew 10:14-15, KJV
And whosoever shall not receive you, or hear your words, when ye depart out of that house or city, shake off the dust of your feet. Verily I say unto you, it shall be more tolerable for the land of Sodom and Gomorrah in the day of judgment than for that city.

Hebrews 10:26-27, NIV

If we deliberately keep on sinning after we have received the knowledge of the truth, no sacrifice for sins is left, but only a fearful expectation of judgment and of raging fire that will consume the enemies of God.

The good news is that God does love us very much. So much that he sent his Son to be a living sacrifice, wiping out the sins of those who believe in him. This is a gift from God, and there is nothing we can do on our own to earn this forgiveness.

Ephesians 2:8-9, NIV

For it is by grace you have been saved, through faith—and this not from yourselves, it is a gift of God—not by works, so that no one can boast. For we are God's workmanship, created in Christ Jesus to do good works, which God prepared in advance for us to do.

It is hard for us to understand the concept of that scripture. We are expected to do good works, but doing them won't save us. Every one of us is a sinner. It is not possible for us to be good enough or do enough good works to earn forgiveness and our way into heaven. It does not matter how much we pray, how much we suffer, how many acts of contrition we perform, we cannot earn forgiveness or work off our sins. No one else on earth can forgive us our sins. It is only by our belief that Jesus is God's Son and that through his sacrifice our sins are no longer seen by God that we are forgiven. If we allow him, God will use us to accomplish many good works, and in fact, he created us with specific works for us to do.

John 3:16-18, HCSB

For God loved the world in this way: He gave his one and only son, so that everyone who believes in him will not perish but have eternal life. For God did not send his son into the world that he might condemn the world, but that the world might be saved through him. Anyone who believes in him is not condemned, but anyone who does not believe is already condemned, because he has not believed in the name of the one and only son of God.

Romans 10:9-11, NLT

For if you confess with your mouth that Jesus is Lord and believe in your heart that God raised him from the dead, you will be saved. For it is by believing in your heart that you are made right with God, and it is by confessing with your mouth that you are saved.

Romans 5:6-9, NASB

For while we were still helpless, at the right time, Christ died for the ungodly. For one will hardly die for a righteous man; though for perhaps for the good man someone would dare even to die. But God demonstrates his own love toward us, in that while we were yet sinners, Christ died for us. Much more then, having been justified by his blood, we shall be saved from the wrath of God through him.

Colossians 1:21-22, HCSB

And you were once alienated and hostile in mind because of your evil actions. But now he has reconciled you by his physical body through his death, to present you holy, faultless, and blameless before him.

1 Timothy 1:15, NIV
Here is a trustworthy saying that deserves full acceptance: Christ Jesus came into the world to save sinners—of whom I am the worst.

Keeping these things in mind, we are now ready to see what the Bible says about homosexuality. I'm including sexual immorality in this topic because the two are almost inseparable. For some reason, the only Bible-based statement that ever makes the news is that God's Word says that marriage should be between a man and a woman. I believe the reason for the use of that scripture is that many states use that terminology to define marriage. That marriage should be between a man and a woman is stated many times throughout the Bible, beginning in Genesis and Leviticus and continuing through Matthew, Corinthians, and Ephesians. Sexual immorality is also found throughout the Bible and appears on almost every list of sinful behavior. As I mentioned in a previous chapter, God distinguishes sexual sins from other sins.

1 Corinthians 6:18, NLT
Run away from sexual sin! No other sin so clearly affects the body as this one does. For sexual immorality is a sin against your own body. Or don't you know that your body is the temple of the Holy Spirit, who lives in you and was given to you by God? You do not belong to yourself, for God bought you with a high price.

Ephesians 5:5-6, NASB
For this you know with certainty, that no immoral or impure person or covetous man, who is an idolater, has an inheritance

in the kingdom of Christ and God. Let no one deceive you with empty words, for because of these things the wrath of God comes upon the sons of disobedience.

1 Corinthians 7:2, HCSB
But because of sexual immorality, each man should have his own wife, and each woman should have her own husband.

Genesis 2:23-25, NLT
"At last!" Adam exclaimed, "She is part of my own flesh and bone!" "She will be called woman, for she was taken out of man." This explains why a man leaves his father and mother and is joined to his wife, and the two are united into one.

Ephesians 5:31, NASB
For this reason a man shall leave his father and mother and shall be joined to his wife, and the two shall become one flesh.

1 Thessalonians 4:3-8, NIV
It is God's will that you should be sanctified; that you should avoid sexual immorality; that each of you should learn to control his own body in a way that is holy and honorable, not in passionate lust like the heathen, who do not know God.

God expresses his feelings about sexual immorality, and in particular homosexuality, more clearly in many other verses though, beginning with the story of Sodom and Gomorrah in the opening book of the Old Testament.

Genesis 18:20, NASB
And the lord said, "The outcry of Sodom and Gomorrah is indeed great, and their sin is exceedingly grave.

The story of Sodom and Gomorrah is pretty long, so I will try to condense it to the

portion that relates to our topic. I recommend that you read Genesis 18:16 through
19:29 so you will know the whole story. To
help you understand the abbreviated portion
of scripture I chose, I will tell you that
God sent two angels to destroy the city of
Sodom, and a man named Lot, fearing for the
angels' safety, had them come into his home.

Genesis 19:4-11, NLT

As they were preparing to retire for the night, all the men of Sodom, young and old, came from all over the city and surrounded the house. They shouted to Lot, "Where are the men who came to spend the night with you? Bring them out so that we can have sex with them." Lot stepped out to talk with them, shutting the door behind him. "Please my brothers," he begged, "don't do such a wicked thing. Look – J have two virgin daughters. Do with them as you wish, but leave these men alone, for they are under my protection." "Stand back!" They shouted. "Who do you think you are? We let you settle among us, and now you are trying to tell us what to do! We'll treat you far worse than those other men!" And they lunged at Lot and began breaking down the door. But the two Angels reached out and pulled Lot in and bolted the door. Then they blinded the men of Sodom so they couldn't find the doorway.

It is said that many forms of sexual immorality were practiced in Sodom and Gomorrah,
including incest and bestiality, but the only
practice clearly stated in these verses is
homosexuality. It was a practice so preva-
lent that the men preferred it to sex with
two young virgin women.

Jude 1:7, NLT
And don't forget the cities of Sodom and Gomorrah and their neighboring towns which were filled with sexual immorality and every kind of sexual perversion. These cities were destroyed by fire and are a warning of the eternal fire that will punish all who are evil.

Leviticus 18:22, NASB
You shall not lie with a male as one lies with a female; it is an abomination.

Leviticus 20:13, NASB
If there is a man who lies with a male as those who lie with a woman, both of them have committed a detestable act; they shall surely be put to death.

If you are homophobic, don't get too excited; you should know that this is only one verse in a long list of immoral acts that called for the death penalty. The list includes things like cursing your father and mother, incest, adultery, bestiality, and many others. God's feelings on homosexuality are continued in the New Testament.

1 Corinthians 6:9–11, NASB
Or do you not know that the unrighteous will not inherit the kingdom of God? Do not be deceived; neither, fornicators, nor idolaters, nor adulterers, nor effeminate, nor homosexuals, nor thieves, nor the covetous, nor drunkards, nor revilers, nor swindlers, will inherit the kingdom of God. Such were some of you; but you were washed, but you were sanctified, but you were justified in the name of the Lord Jesus Christ and in the spirit of our God.

I had to include the whole list to keep all of us from self-righteousness. That list isn't even close to being exhaustive either. There are many lists of things detestable to God throughout the Bible. None of those lists are meant to be the entirety of what God views as sinful. Each list contains the particular items that those who heard it needed to hear and were struggling with. Please take note that all of those sinners on that list were washed of their sins when they accepted Christ as their savior. In Corinth, in particular, many immoral sexual practices were taking place both with Christians and non-Christians alike. According to the *International Inductive Study Bible*, immorality was so blatant in Corinth that the term "to Corinthianize" meant to practice sexual immorality. Prostitution was common and even practiced in churches there. The *IISB* states that the Temple of Aphrodite had a worship ceremony carried out by a thousand temple prostitutes. Paul addressed it with the following verses.

1 Corinthians 6:15–16, NLT
Don't you realize that your bodies are actually parts of Christ? Should a man take his body, which belongs to Christ, and join it to a prostitute? Never! And don't you know that if a man joins himself to a prostitute, he becomes one body with her? For the scriptures say "The two are united into one."

Prostitution was a practice of the ungodly throughout the Bible, with male prostitution being mentioned in particular in 1 Kings.

1 Kings 14:24, NASB
There were also cult male prostitutes in the land. They did according to all the abominations of the nations, which the Lord dispossessed before the sons of Israel.

You may be surprised to know that cross-dressing is also mentioned in the Bible, as is bestiality, or sex with animals.

Deuteronomy 22:5, NASB
A woman shall not wear man's clothing, nor shall a man put on woman's clothing; for whoever does these things is an abomination to the Lord your God.

Leviticus 18:23, NLT
A man must never defile himself by having sexual intercourse with an animal, and a woman must never present herself to a male animal in order to have intercourse with it; this is a terrible perversion.

The clearest expression of God's feelings concerning homosexuality, and the final verses that I intend to use, are found in Romans. I'm afraid it is long, but I think that I have to include the whole thing. I'm using the New Living Translation because it is clear and easily understood, using the language of our day. I encourage you to read other versions to affirm this one.

Romans 1:21-32, NLT
Yes, they knew God, but they wouldn't worship him as God or even give him thanks. And they began to think up foolish ideas of what God was like. The result was that their minds became dark and confused. Claiming to be wise, they became utter fools instead. And instead of worshiping the glorious,

ever-living God, they worshiped idols made to look like mere people, or birds and animals and snakes.

So God let them go ahead and do whatever shameful things their hearts desired. As a result they did vile and degrading things with each other's bodies. Instead of believing what they knew was the truth about God, they deliberately chose to believe lies. So they worshiped the things God made but not the Creator himself, who is to be praised forever Amen.

That is why God abandoned them to their shameful desires. Even the women turned against the natural way to have sex and instead indulged in sex with each other. And the men, instead of having normal sexual relationships with women, burned with lust for each other. Men did shameful things with other men and, as a result, suffered within themselves the penalty they so richly deserved.

When they refused to acknowledge God, he abandoned them to their evil minds and let them do things that should never be done. Their lives became full of every kind of wickedness sin, greed, hate, envy, murder, fighting, deception, malicious behavior, and gossip. They are backstabbers, haters of God, insolent, proud, and boastful. They are forever inventing new ways of sinning and are disobedient to their parents. They refuse to understand, break their promises, and are heartless and unforgiving. They are fully aware of God's death penalty for those who do these things, yet they go right ahead and do them anyway. And, worse yet, they encourage others to do them too.

Paul follows up those verses with some more very powerful verses that bring us back to the reality that we are all sinners. All of us need to get our act together and straighten up. There is a very big dan-

71

ger when we focus on the sins of others and become blind to our own. I am switching to The New American Standard Bible for these verses, but they follow directly after those listed previously. This is very long also, but it is worth it.

Romans 2:1-11, NASB

Therefore you have no excuse, every one of you who passes judgment, for in that which you judge another you condemn yourself; for you who judge practice the same things. And we know that the judgment of God rightly falls upon those who practice such things. But do you suppose this, O man, when you pass judgment on those who practice such things and do the same yourself, that you will escape the judgment of God? Or do you think lightly of the riches of his kindness and tolerance and patience, not knowing that the kindness of God leads you to repentance?

These verses, along with several others in scripture, are taken by many to mean that we should all just leave each other alone and we shouldn't judge each other. There is a difference between judging each other and passing judgment. We are all sinners, and the church is full of sinners. You should not pass judgment or condemn someone else to hell when you are a sinner yourself. "Let he who is without sin cast the first stone," and "take the log out of your own eye before you try to take the speck out of your brother's eye." However, we are supposed to use our own judgment, or discernment, to recognize our brother's sin in order to help lovingly restore him.

Galatians 6:1-2, NASB

Dear brothers and sisters, if another Christian is overcome by some sin, you who are godly should gently and humbly help that person back onto the right path. And be careful not to fall into the same temptation yourself. Share each other's troubles and problems, and in this way obey the laws of Christ.

All Christians who have given their heart to God are godly. The strength of the church is that I may be able to help someone fight his battle with sin by lovingly helping him back on the right path, while someone else helps me fight my own demons.

The only conclusion possible, if we accept that scripture comes from God, is that God considers homosexuality a sin. I do not claim in any way to understand why. All of us know women who are clearly born with masculine features and characteristics. We also know men who are clearly effeminate and have always been that way. Why God would create people that way and then condemn that lifestyle is beyond my ability to explain. There are a multitude of people, however, who have turned to a homosexual lifestyle for other reasons. Sexual molestation during childhood has a devastating effect on the human psyche and adulthood behavior, one of which is same-sex attraction. Mental and physical abuse, severe blows to self-esteem, feeling unloved and rejected by the opposite sex, and sex addiction also drive people into same-sex relationships. God's wisdom is far beyond my understanding. I feel compassion for those who say, "But God created me this way." As has been stated before, though, there are many seriously addictive sins involving drugs, alcohol, gambling, and sex that cause us to say the same thing. I can only show you what scripture says. What I do know is that churches cannot shut their doors to homosexuals any more than they can to any other sinner. Because of their compassion, many churches have decreed that homosexuality is an acceptable lifestyle and have welcomed practicing gays and lesbians into their leadership and ministry. I would caution the leadership of those churches that they are not teaching what God says through scripture, and their compassion, while helping homosexuals find worldly acceptance, may cost homosexuals eternally.

Ephesians 5:5-7, NIV
For of this you can be sure: No immoral, impure, or greedy person- such a man is an idolater- has any inheritance in the Kingdom of Christ and God. Let no one deceive you with empty words, for because of such things God's wrath comes on those who are disobedient. Therefore do not be partners with them.

James 3:1, NASB
Let not many of you become teachers, my brethren, knowing that as such we shall incur a stricter judgment.

Teaching something that is contrary to scripture, no matter how good your intentions are, is a dangerous practice, especially if an entire denomination or church body is being led astray.

1 Timothy 1:5-11, HCSB

Now the goal of our instruction is love from a pure heart, a good conscience, and a sincere faith. Some have deviated from these and turned aside to fruitless discussion. They want to be teachers of the law, although they don't understand what they are saying or what they are insisting on. Now we know that the law is good, provided one uses it legitimately. We know that the law is not meant for the righteous person, but for the lawless and rebellious, for the ungodly and sinful, for the unholy and irreverent, for those who kill their fathers and mothers, for murderers, for the sexually immoral and homosexuals, for kidnapers, liars, perjurers, and for whatever else is contrary to the sound teaching based on the glorious gospel of the blessed God that was entrusted to me.

Mark 7:6-8, NLT

Jesus replied, "You hypocrites! Isaiah was prophesying about you when he said. These people honor me with their lips, but their hearts are far away. Their worship is a farce, for they replace God's commands with their own man-made teachings. For you ignore God's specific laws and substitute your own traditions.

I suppose I could place these last few scriptures at the end of every chapter. It seems that we are either teaching that something is a sin when it isn't or teaching that it is not a sin when it is. My reason for writing this book is to try to bring the divisions we have created through our various denominations to an end. God did not intend it to be that way. Just because we have labeled ourselves a church does not mean that God approves. There will be many churches and church attendees who will not be recognized by God when he brings things to a close. If

I've learned anything through this study, it is that we will be judged by our hearts. I am not implying that the plan of salvation outlined through scripture doesn't matter. I am not saying that belief in the one true God, belief that your sins are forgiven through Christ's sacrificial blood, confessing your sins to God, repenting of those sins, and dying to your old self through baptism are not necessary. Your salvation will not be achieved simply by having a good heart. What I am saying is that your heart will expose your motivation for all that you have done in the name of God. It will not matter how godly we have looked to men, how many times we have attended church, or how many good deeds we have done. What will matter is why you did those things and whether you will jump for joy at the sight of Jesus upon his return. It will not be that difficult for God to judge us; our hearts will be exposed for all to see.

2 Timothy 4:7-8, KJV
I have fought the good fight, I have finished my course, I have kept the faith: Henceforth there is laid up for me a crown of righteousness, which the Lord, the righteous judge, shall give me at that day: and not to me only, but unto all them also that love his appearing.

We will be severely judged as teachers and church leaders if we continue to confuse and frustrate God's children. I accept that I may be wrong in my interpretation of scripture. If through your own study of God's Word you can show me to be wrong, I will thank you.

My only desire is to find the truth of God's Word. But if you base your disagreements on what others have told you, the traditions in which you were brought up, or your own feelings, you may want to rethink your position.

Proverbs 30:5-6, HCSB
Every word of God is pure; He is a shield to those who take refuge in him. Don't add to his words, or he will rebuke you and you will be proved a liar.

Matthew 22:29, HCSB
Jesus answered them, "You are deceived, because you don't know the scriptures or the power of God.

You would think Jesus is talking to people uneducated in scripture when he said that, but in fact, he was talking to the Sadducees, who were the leaders of a sect of Jews who did not believe in resurrection. They were very respected and powerful and held the same status as the Pharisees.

Chapter 11

Priest and Marriage

The idea that a priest should not be married comes from the teachings of Paul. Paul was never married and urged others to remain unmarried so they could devote themselves more fully to God.

1 Corinthians 7:1, NLT
Now about the questions you asked in your letter. Yes, it is good to live a celibate life.

1 Corinthians 7:7, NLT
I wish everyone could get along without marrying, just as I do. But we are not all the same. God gives some the gift of marriage, and to others he gives the gift of singleness.

1 Corinthians 7:8-9, NLT
Now I say to those who aren't married and to widows- it's better to stay unmarried, just as I am. But if they can't control themselves, they should go ahead and marry. It's better to marry than to burn with lust.

Paul was speaking to everyone in these verses, but the most probable reason his suggestion was directed to church leaders, both male and female, is found in verse 32 of the same chapter, where he explains why it is better to be single.

1 Corinthians 7:32-35, NLT

In everything you do I want you to be free from the concerns of this life. An unmarried man can spend his time doing the Lord's work and thinking how to please him. But a married man can't do that so well. He has to think about his earthly responsibilities and how to please his wife. His interests are divided. In the same way, a woman who is no longer married or has never been married can be more devoted to the Lord in body and spirit, while the married woman must be concerned about her earthly responsibilities and how to please her husband. I am saying this for your benefit, and not to place restrictions on you. I want you to do whatever will help you to serve the Lord best, with as few distractions as possible. But if a man thinks he ought to marry his fiancée because he has trouble controlling his passions and time is passing, it is all right; it is not a sin. Let them marry. But if he decides firmly not to marry and there is no urgency and he can control his passion, he does well not to marry. So the person who marries does well, and the person who doesn't marry does even better.

It is easy to see why a heavy push would be made to require the head of a church and those serving the church to remain single, allowing them to devote their undivided attention to serving God. Paul, however, clearly states in verse 36 that if you feel you have to marry, it is all right; it is not a sin. There are several verses in the Old Testament that discuss the marriage of priests.

Leviticus 21:7, NIV
They must not marry women defiled by prostitution or divorced from their husbands, because priests are holy to their God.

Leviticus 21:9, NIV
If a Priest daughter defiles herself by becoming a prostitute, she disgraces her father; she must be burned in the fire.

Leviticus 21:13, NIV
The woman he marries must be a virgin.

Obviously a discussion about the type of wives a priest should have and how priests' daughters should act implies that they were married. Still the argument can be made that the Old Testament teachings for Jewish priests do not apply to Christian priests. It is a very good argument, since the lifestyle of many of the Jewish church leaders was severely admonished by Jesus. Jesus himself did not mention marriage by church leaders. Most of his apostles eventually married. Paul was an exception, not the norm. In Matthew, we are told that Peter was married even before Christ was crucified. The verses do not mention Peter's wife, but they do speak of his mother-in-law whom Jesus healed.

Matthew 8:14-15, NASB
When Jesus came into Peter's home, he saw his mother-in-law lying sick in bed with fever. He touched her hand, and the fever left her; and she got up and waited on him.

Not only does Paul directly say it is not a sin to be married, but Jesus obviously did not feel compelled to restrict his apostles from marriage. While there is no doubt that it would be beneficial to the church for its leaders to be single and devote their lives to serving God, it is not a command that comes from God. It is by far more devastating to the church for their leaders to burn with lust and to lose control of themselves than for them to be married.

Chapter 12

Sorcery, Magic, Fortune-Telling, Tattooing, Etc.

It is fashionable for many to talk to spiritual mediums or go to séances to try to make contact with the dead. It is playful and fun to mess with Ouija boards or go to fortune-tellers to see what our future might hold. But I think the majority of us will be surprised to see what God's Word has to say about those things. What often passes for amusement today was taken very seriously historically. Seeking spiritual guidance from anyone other than God is considered idolatry.

Deuteronomy 18:9-14, HCSB
When you enter the land the Lord your God is giving you, do not imitate the detestable customs of those nations. No one among you is to make his son or daughter pass through the fire, practice divination, tell fortunes, interpret omens, practice sorcery, cast spells, consult a medium or a familiar spirit, or inquire of the dead. Everyone who does these things is detestable to the Lord, and the Lord your God is driving out the nations before you because of these detestable things.

Leviticus 19:26, NLT
Never eat meat that has not been drained of its blood. Do not practice fortune telling or witchcraft.

The other translations use "divination," "sorcery," and "soothsaying."

Leviticus 19:28, NIV
Do not cut your bodies for the dead or put tattoo marks on yourselves. I am the Lord.

Leviticus 19:31, NASB
Do not turn to mediums or spiritists; do not seek them out to be defiled by them. I am the Lord your God.

The New Living Translation uses the word "psychics" in place of "spiritists."

Leviticus 20:6, KJV
And the soul that turneth after such as have familiar spirits, and after wizards, to go whoring after them, I will even set my face against that soul, and I will cut him off from among his people.

2 Chronicles 33:6, NASB
And he made his sons pass through the fire in the valley of Benhinnom; and he practiced witchcraft, used divination, practiced sorcery, and dealt with mediums and spiritists. He did much evil in the site of the Lord, provoking him to anger.

Revelation 21:8, NASB
But for the cowardly and unbelieving and abominable and murderers and immoral persons and sorcerers and idolaters and all liars, their part will be in the lake that burns with fire and brimstone, which is the second death.

There are more verses on this topic, but I think there are enough here to make it clear we are not to participate in anything that has to do with spirituality unless it is through God. Voodoo is not mentioned in the Bible, but I am convinced it would be included in the list of sinful behaviors. I believe that tattooing was heavily associated with the people who practiced these black arts. There are those in the world today that link their tattoos and piercings to satan and the practice of black arts. My opinion, though, is that the practice of tattooing for the majority of people today is so far removed from that association that having one is not sinful. Don't take my word for it though. I do not have a biblical basis to back that up.

Chapter 13

Dancing, Music, Instruments, and Singing

I almost don't know what to say when it comes to churches that restrict or forbid these activities. The Bible is full of examples where Christians are doing all of these things to raise a joyful noise to the Lord. Throughout the Bible, these things are used as a part of worship or in Christian celebration. In Nehemiah 12, we see the story of a celebration because the Jews finished restoring the walls of Jerusalem. The story goes from verse 27 through verse 47. It is too long to include the whole thing, so I am doing something I haven't done yet; I am taking snippets here and there throughout those verses. You can double-check me by reading the whole thing.

Nehemiah 12:27-47, NIV

At the dedication . . . Levites were . . . brought to Jerusalem to celebrate joyfully the dedication with songs of thanksgiving and with the music of cymbals, harps, and lyres. I also assigned two large choirs to give thanks . . . as well as some priest with trumpets . . . with musical instruments pre-

scribed by David the man of God. The sound of rejoicing in Jerusalem could be heard from far away.

1 Chronicles 16:42, NLT
They used their trumpets, cymbals, and other instruments to accompany the songs of praise to God.

Psalms 33:1-3, NIV
Sing joyfully to the Lord, you righteous; it is fitting for the upright to praise him. Praise the Lord with the harp; make music to him on the 10 stringed lyre. Sing to him a new song; play skillfully, and shout for joy.

Psalms 98:4-6, KJV
Make a joyful noise unto the Lord, all the earth: Make a loud noise, and rejoice, and sing praise. Sing unto the Lord with the harp; with the harp and the voice of Psalm, with Trumpets and sound of Cornet make a joyful noise before the Lord, the King.

Ephesians 5:19, NIV
Speak to one another with Psalms, hymns, and spiritual songs.

Colossians 3:16, NLT
Sing Psalms and hymns and spiritual songs to God with thankful hearts.

Exodus 15:20, NIV
Then Miriam the prophetess, Aaron's sister, took a tambourine in her hand, and all the women followed her, with tambourines and dancing.

2 Samuel 6:14, NASB
And David was dancing before the Lord with all his might, and David was wearing a linen ephod.

Luke 15:25, NASB
Now his older son was in the field, and when he came and approached the house, he heard music and dancing.

Music, song, and dance are all used to praise and celebrate God's glory. I'm pretty sure he enjoys it. He filled us with the ability, and he asked us to do it. None of those things are sinful.

Chapter 14

Anger, Slander, Dissension, Gossip, Lying, Etc.

This is a pretty broad group of topics to cobble together. There are so many scriptures related to anger that it could easily have had a chapter of its own. Almost every sin known to man is in some way tied to lying. You can't commit a sin of any kind without lying about it to someone. For the sake of brevity, I will keep them together. I will also include scripture about the tongue in this chapter because it is the weapon of choice when committing these kinds of sins. In some of the lists of sins that God hates, he includes murder as part of the group. That may seem odd, but in reality, anyone sinning in one of these ways is generally trying to destroy someone with the power of the tongue. Grouping all of these together means that there will probably be more scripture included than you want to look at. If I did each topic individually, however, I'm sure that I would wear you out even more. Please bear with me.

Proverbs 6:16–19, NIV
There are six things that the Lord hates, seven that are detestable to him: haughty eyes, a lying tongue, hands that shed innocent blood, a heart that devises wicked schemes, feet that are quick to rush into evil, a false witness that pours out lies and a man that stirs up dissention among brothers.

"Haughty" isn't a common word today, so I'll include a definition from the *Oxford* dictionary, "high in one's own estimation; proud, arrogant, supercilious." The easiest way to look at it may be as the opposite of being humble.

Proverbs 11:9, NASB
With his mouth the godless man destroys his neighbor, but through knowledge the righteous will be delivered.

Proverbs 14:17, NLT
Those who are short tempered do foolish things, and schemers are hated.

Proverbs 15:18, NIV
A hot tempered man stirs up dissension, but a patient man calms a quarrel.

Proverbs 22:24–25, HCSB
Don't make friends with an angry man, and don't be a companion of a hot-tempered man, or you will learn his ways and entangle yourself in a snare.

Ephesians 4:31–32, NLT
Get rid of all bitterness, rage, anger, harsh words, and slander, as well as all types of malicious behavior. Instead be kind to each other, tenderhearted, forgiving one another, just as God through Jesus has forgiven you.

Colossians 3:8, NIV

But now you must rid yourself of all such things as these: anger, rage, malice, slander, and filthy language from your lips.

1 Peter 2:1, NLT

So get rid of all malicious behavior and deceit. Don't just pretend to be good! Be done with hypocrisy and jealousy and back stabbing.

1 John 4:20, NASB

If someone says, "I love God," and hates his brother, he is a liar; for the one who does not love his brother whom he has seen, cannot love God whom he has not seen.

James 3:5-8, NIV

Likewise the tongue is a small part of the body, but it makes great boast. Consider what a great forest is set on fire by a small spark. The tongue is also a fire, a world of evil among the parts of the body. It corrupts the whole person, sets the whole course of his life on fire, and is itself set on fire by hell. All kinds of animals, birds, reptiles and creatures of the sea are being tamed and have been tamed by man, but no man can tame the tongue. It is a restless evil, full of deadly poison.

James 2:26, NLT

If you claim to be religious but don't control your tongue, you are just fooling yourself, and your religion is worthless.

Psalms 101:5, NLT

I will not tolerate people who slander their neighbors; I will not endure conceit and pride.

Psalms 101:7, NLT

I will not allow deceivers to serve me and liars will not be allowed to enter my presence.

The sins I have listed in this group tend to be deemed as largely harmless by most of us. We do not have a big problem with justifying a lie now and then, taking our employer's property when we need it, passing on some juicy gossip, or slandering someone's reputation if we don't like them. We surely don't put them on the same level as committing adultery or murder. God, however, hates all of these the same as he hates murder. Surprisingly, anger is the only thing in this group that God makes allowances for. Jesus himself angrily turned over the tables of the vendors who were using the requirement to sacrifice as a way to extort money from worshipers. They created laws requiring items to be sacrificed that only they could provide and then charged exorbitant fees for them. His anger was powerful enough that he was able to run them right out of the temple. What God says in James 1:19 is to be slow to anger. In Ephesians 4:26, he says to be angry, but do not sin, and not let the sun go down on our anger. It is only those who wallow in their anger and can't get past it that we are to avoid. What God finds detestable about these sins is that they tear apart the body of the church. Lies, slander, anger, false witness, and gossip are all used by Christians to create division in the body and to promote personal agendas. These sins cannot be allowed to go unchecked, and God has given individual Christians and church leadership the responsibility of ending that behavior.

Matthew 18:13–17, NLT

If another believer sins against you, go privately and point out the fault. If the other person listens and confesses it, you have won that person back. But if you are unsuccessful, take one or two others with you and go back again, so that everything you say may be confirmed by two or three witnesses. If that person still refuses to listen, take your case to the church. If the church decides you are right, but the other person won't accept it, treat that person as a pagan or a corrupt tax collector.

Romans 15:14, KJV

And I myself also am persuaded of you, my brethren, that ye also are full of goodness, filled with all knowledge, able also to admonish one another.

Romans 16:17–18, NIV

I urge you, brothers, to watch out for those who cause divisions and put obstacles in your way that are contrary to the teaching you have learned. Keep away from them, for such people are not serving our Lord Christ, but their own appetites. By smooth talk and flattery they deceive the minds of naïve people.

The term "naïve people" was not derogatory, but only meant to describe the innocence of the multitude of newborn Christians in that day. Their world was full of people trying to lead them back to Judaism or to adulterated versions of Christianity. These adulterated versions did not come from God but rather from men. Unfortunately we have the same practices continuing today, which have resulted in a multitude of denominations and a state of confusion for Christians. My desire is that all of God's people would read and study scripture for themselves and refrain from allowing other people to tell them what God desires. You should know that I include myself and this book in that statement. Don't take my word for any of this but allow God to bring you understanding as you study his Word. Now back to the topic at hand.

1 Corinthians 5:1-2, NLT

I can hardly believe the report about the sexual immorality going on among you, something so evil that even the pagans don't do it. I am told that you have a man in your church who is living in sin with his father's wife. And you are so proud of yourselves! Why aren't you mourning in sorrow and shame? And why haven't you removed this man from your fellowship?

I included this scripture even though it is about sexual immorality because the church body is directed to treat this sin in the same way as the sins in our topic. God sees them the same, and it creates the same problem for the church body.

1 Corinthians 5:6-7a, NLT

How terrible that you should boast about your spirituality, and yet you let this sort of thing go on. Don't you realize that if even one person is allowed to go on sinning, soon all will be affected? Remove this wicked person from among you so that you can stay pure.

I know that whether or not we are supposed to judge other people, when we are sinners ourselves, is a problem for us. What God is talking about here is blatant and unrepentant sin that is affecting the rest of the body. If church leadership allows that kind of behavior to continue, it will eventually be viewed as acceptable by the body, and others will be led astray. It would be good for you to read the whole chapter and all of chapter 6 in 1 Corinthians. Chapter 5 goes on to clarify the difference between judging other Christians and judging non-Christians. I'm afraid it is rather long, but I think it is important.

1 Corinthians 5:6-13, NLT

When I wrote to you before, I told you not to associate with people who indulge in sexual sin. But I wasn't talking about unbelievers who indulge in sexual sin, or who are greedy or are swindlers or idol worshipers. You would have to leave this world to avoid people like that. What I meant was that you are not to associate with anyone who claims to be a Christian yet indulges in sexual sin, or is greedy, or worships idols, or is abusive, or a drunkard, or a swindler. Don't even eat with such people. It isn't my responsibility to judge outsiders, but it certainly is your job to judge those inside the church who are sinning in these ways. God will judge those on the outside; but as the scriptures say, you must remove the evil person from among you.

Scripture also emphasizes that we should make every effort to help a fellow Christian realize that he is not living as he should and give him the opportunity to repent. The only way one sinner can do this with another sinner is if it is done in love and there is true concern and compassion for your fellow Christian's soul.

Galatians 6:1, NIV
Brothers, if someone is caught in a sin, you who are spiritual should restore him gently. But watch yourself or you also may be tempted.

Titus 3:10, NIV
Warn a divisive person once, and then warn him a second time. After that, have nothing to do with him.

James 5:19-20, NASB
My brethren, if any among you strays from the truth and one turns him back, let him know that he who turns a sinner from the error of his way will save his soul from death and will cover a multitude of sins.

If you care to read Hebrews 12, you will find many scriptures about discipline. God disciplines us because he loves us and he is trying to lead us in the right direction. Being disciplined is never pleasant when it takes place, but as we know with our own children, the end result is worth it. I have given you so much scripture in this chapter already that I choose not to add to it even though understanding how much you are loved by God is more important than anything else I have written. He loves you in a powerful way that you will never completely know until he is able to shower you with it in heaven.

Chapter 15

Tithing

I believe that the idea of the failure to tithe as being a sin is something that most Christians don't think about. In our modern view of religion, we tend to view it as an option if we can afford it and feel like doing it. One of the biggest criticisms from non-Christians is that it seems the main thing churches want is money. Even many of us who call ourselves Christians find being encouraged to give unpleasant. The idea of giving 10 percent of our income is almost offensive to us, and very few actually do it. The standard rule of thumb followed by church leadership is that 10 percent of the body accounts for 90 percent of the giving. The same rule of thumb applies to the church members who teach, visit, clean, cook, or do any other work that allows churches to operate. Ten percent of the church body generally does about 90 percent of the work. Sadly, it is not unusual for many of the same people who give to also be the ones doing the work. I know that there are always new Christians in any church body and that they are still growing in their faith, but that still leaves a huge number of believers who feel they cannot afford to give either physically or financially. Even though churches require money to operate, the idea of tithing did not come from them. God established tithing with Adam and Eve, and there is more scripture found on giving than any other subject in the Bible. You will see in the scriptures to follow that God uses our willingness to sacrifice as a test of our love for him.

Genesis 4:2-6, NIV

Now Abel kept flocks and Cain worked the soil. In the course of time Cain brought some of the fruits of the soil as an offering to the lord. But Abel brought fat portions from some of the firstborn of his flock. The Lord looked with favor on Abel and his offering, but on Cain and his offering he did not look with favor. So Cain was very angry and his face was downcast. Then the lord said to Cain, "Why are you angry? Why is your face downcast? If you do what is right will you not be accepted? But if you do not do what is right sin is crouching at your door; it desires to have you but you must master it."

You have to read this brief scripture closely to really understand what is going on. Abel did not hold back; he brought the very best portions that he had from his healthiest firstborn animals. Firstborn is important because he didn't wait to see if he would be able to spare it. He placed his faith in God to take care of his needs. Cain, on the other hand, "brought some of the fruits of the soil." He held back. He saved the best, the richest, the plumpest first fruits of his crop for himself. Sin indeed was crouching at his door because his anger and jealously led him to kill his own brother.

Matthew 6:19–21, NLT

Don't store up treasures here on earth, where they can be eaten by moths and get rusty, and where thieves break in and steal. Store your treasures in heaven, where they will never become moth-eaten or rusty and where they will be safe from thieves. Wherever your treasure is, there your heart and thoughts will be also.

Wherever your treasure is, your heart and thoughts will be also. In the same chapter only a verse or two later, God clearly tells us how he feels about our desire for money.

Matthew 6:24, NLT

No one can serve two masters. For you will hate one and love the other, or be devoted to one and despise the other. You cannot serve both God and money.

The rest of chapter 6 goes on to tell us that we need to quit relying on our own abilities and possessions for our well-being and rely on God instead. If you take the time to read the whole chapter, you will have a better understanding of what I am trying to say to you. God wants us to trust him, to rely on him, to put our faith in him completely. If we are reluctant to give 10 percent of what God has given us back to him, we are clearly showing him that the world carries far more importance to us than our faith in him. It is not money that is the problem but our love of money. More than that, it is our self-centered lifestyle that says taking care of ourselves is the most important thing there is. We cannot be used by God if we selfishly hoard the blessings he gives us.

Ecclesiastes 5:10, NIV

Whoever loves money never has money enough; whoever loves wealth is never satisfied with his income. This too is meaningless.

1 Timothy 6:6–10, NASB

But Godliness actually is a means of great gain when accompanied by contentment. For we have brought nothing into the world, so we cannot take anything out of it either. If we have food and covering, with these we shall be content. But those who want to get rich fall into temptation and a snare and many foolish and harmful desires which plunge men into ruin and destruction. For the love of money is a root of all sorts of evil, and some by longing for it have wandered away from the faith and pierced themselves with many griefs.

Please note that God's Word does not say, "Money is the root of all evil," but rather, "The love of money is a root of many kinds of evil."

1 Timothy 6:17–19, NLT

Tell those who are rich in this world not to be proud and not to trust in their money, which will soon be gone. But their trust should be in the living God, who richly gives us all we need for our enjoyment. Tell them to use their money to do good. They should be rich in good works and should give generously to those in need, always being ready to share with others whatever God has given them. By doing this they will be storing up their treasure as a good foundation for the future so that they may take hold of real life.

As discussed in previous chapters, God created each of us for a purpose. He blesses us with gifts, talents, wisdom, or wealth so he can use us to bless others, bringing them to know the love of God. If we choke off his flow of blessings by hoarding them all for ourselves, he cannot work through us. When our desire for wealth becomes more important than God, we have turned money into an idol.

Biblically, a tithe is 10 percent of whatever God has blessed you with. The first question all of us have as new Christians is, "Are we talking net income or gross income?" The short answer is your gross income. God asks for the first fruits of your blessings. If we truly are putting our faith in God to take care of us, then sacrificing the money is not a burden but a source of contentment. The way we cling to our money is an easy way for God to know where we stand with our faith in him. God knows our hearts; we can fake it with the rest of the world, but the motivation of our heart will be exposed before God. I have to admit that I struggled to come to grips with giving 10 percent of my gross income for many years as I matured as a Christian. What I finally realized about myself was that I couldn't get myself to give God the money because I felt I needed it to take care of myself and my family; I was relying on myself. In addition to that, there was always a house to buy, a car, a TV, a vacation, or some other "need" to take care of. I rarely had any extra money to give. It was only when I learned to give God the first fruits, instead of part of what I had left, that tithing ceased to be a burden. Once you get used to giving God the first 10 percent, you learn to trust God to help you live on the 90 percent you have left.

Proverbs 3:9-10, NASB
Honor the Lord from you wealth, and from the first of all of your produce; so your barns will be filled with plenty, and your vats will overflow with new wine.

Not only does God tell us to give of our first fruits, but he also says that he will bless us with more fruits if we do. Unfortunately, a misguided denomination has sprouted up based on the belief that God will make you prosperous if you give enough. If your only motive for giving is to get rich, you will be disappointed. If you allow him, God will do his work through you. If he blesses the giving of your wealth, then he provides you with even more wealth to give. You will find that you cannot outgive God. I know a man who continually increased his giving because he found that he always had enough to live on. He is now at a point in his life that he is giving 90 percent of his income away and living on 10 percent. The following is another very interesting passage. In fact, I had never heard it before doing research for this book.

Deuteronomy 14:22-27, NIV
Be sure to set aside a tenth of all that your fields produce each year. Eat the tithe of your grain, new wine and oil, and the first born of your herds and flocks in the presence of the Lord your God at the place he will choose as a dwelling for

his name, so that you may learn to revere the *Lord* your *God* always. *But* if the place is too distant and you have been blessed by the lord your *God* and cannot carry your tithe then exchange your tithe for silver, and take the silver with you and go to the place the *Lord* your *God* will choose. *Use* the silver to buy whatever you like: cattle, sheep, wine or other fermented drink, or anything you wish. *Then* you and your household shall eat there in the presence of the *Lord* your *God* and rejoice. *And* do not neglect the *Levites* living in your towns, for they have no allotment or inheritance of their own.

This scripture says to bring your tithe to show your reverence or your fear of the Lord. Then it says that you and your family should eat your tithe in the Lord's presence and rejoice. I should have used this in the chapter on drinking because it also clearly gives permission to drink alcohol. Enjoy fellowshipping over a meal with God; I think that gives us an amazing insight into how much God loves us and enjoys our company. It is interesting to note that the pilgrims followed the intent of this scripture when they celebrated the first Thanksgiving, and we continue that tradition today. The tithe was established with Adam as a way of honoring God. Scripture goes on to say that we should take care of those who serve the Lord full time. Financing the church staff and the operation of the church was the typical use for tithes from the beginning and still is today. It's funny because my compassion wants to say that failing to tithe is not sinful. Scripture throughout the Bible, however, clearly shows that God expects it. God does not give us an option; therefore, we are sinning when we do not honor God with our tithe. What our reluctance or failure to fully tithe does is give God an easy insight into our heart. Do you trust in your own ability to take care of yourself and your family, or do you trust in God? My final comment on tithing is from my personal belief that your tithe has very little to do with the needs of the church. Your tithe is a commitment to God. When you commit to God to give a *first fruits* tithe, you are agreeing to give 10 percent of your income up-front and living on whatever you have remaining. By doing that, you must trust God and depend on him to take care of you. The only way church needs should affect your giving is if you decide to give more than your committed tithe.

Chapter 16

Baptism

This will be the final chapter in this book, which may bring a sigh of relief to many of you. I have decided to include it because the need to be baptized and the method of baptism are a source of division in today's religions. Denominations teach everything from baptism by immersion, to sprinkling, to being saved by faith alone without being baptized. The changes in baptism came into effect over many years, but in Jesus's day, everyone who became a Christ follower was baptized by immersion. Jesus himself was baptized in this way and instructed his disciples to baptize believers in the name of the Father and the Son and the Holy Spirit. We must all understand though that God is all-powerful, omnipotent, and answers to no one. He can and does do whatever he wishes. No one can say that those who were not baptized or were not immersed will not go to heaven. Clearly the thief crucified with Jesus was not baptized yet was promised that he would see Jesus in heaven. While there are a very limited number of scriptures that mention becoming a Christian without mentioning baptism, the overwhelming majority profess it as a necessary part of the process. Scripture tells us to be baptized for the forgiveness of our sins. Scripture also tells us that the sacrifice of Jesus and his shed blood covers our sin. The link between the shed blood of Jesus and the act of baptism is seldom discussed, but it does exist. Accepting Jesus as your savior and believing that his blood was shed for the forgiveness of your sins always precedes baptism. The act of baptism then demonstrates to the world that you are willing to die to your old life of sin, be buried in a watery grave, and rise from that grave with a new life as pure and undefiled as your original birth. It is in this new pure state that you are able to receive the Holy Spirit.

Mark 10:38, KJV; italics by the author
But Jesus said to them, "You do not know what you are asking. Are you able to drink the cup that I drink, or to be baptized with the baptism with which I am baptized?"

Luke 12:50, NLT
There is a terrible baptism ahead of me, and I am under a heavy burden until it is accomplished.

John 19:34, KJV
But one of the soldiers with a spear pierced his side, and forthwith came there out blood and water.

1 John 5:4-8, NLT
For every child of God defeats this evil world by trusting Christ to give the victory. And the ones who win this battle against the world are the ones who believe that Jesus is the Son of God. And Jesus Christ was revealed as God's

Son by his baptism in water and by shedding his blood on the cross—not by water only, but by water and blood. And the Spirit also gives us the testimony that this is true. So we have three witnesses—the Spirit, the water and the blood—and all three agree.

None of the other bible versions mention "his baptism in water." They all simply say that Jesus is the one who came by water and blood. Until my study for this book, I assumed that the water being referred to was the water that resulted from the piercing of Christ's side. I still feel that this water represents baptism. God clearly identified Jesus as his son after his baptism by water, so perhaps the water and blood coming from his side represented the two baptisms of Christ. Regardless, there is a very strong link between baptism and the crucifixion.

Hebrews 9:27, NIV
Just as man is destined to die once, and after that to face judgment, so Christ was sacrificed once to take away the sins of many people; and he will appear a second time, not to bear sin, but to bring salvation to those who are waiting for him.

Matthew 3:13-17, NASB
Then Jesus arrived from Galilee at the Jordan coming to John to be baptized by him. But John tried to prevent him, saying, "I have need to be baptized by you, and do you come to me?" But Jesus answering said to him, "Permit it at this time, for in this way it is fitting for us to fulfill all righteousness." Then he permitted him. After being baptized, Jesus came up immediately from the water; and behold, the heavens were opened, and he saw the Spirit of God descending as a dove and lighting on him, and behold, a voice out of the heav-

ens said, "This is My beloved Son, in whom J am well pleased."

There is little argument here, but it should be noted that Jesus "came up immediately out of the water" and was therefore immersed.

Matthew 28:18-20, NASB

And Jesus came up and spoke to them, saying, "All authority has been given to me in heaven and earth. Go therefore and make disciples of all nations, baptizing them in the name of the Father, and the Son, and the Holy Spirit. Teaching them to obey everything J have commanded you; and lo J am with you always, even to the end of the age.

Romans 6:1-5, HCSB

What should we say then? Should we continue to sin in order that grace may multiply? Absolutely not! How can we who died to sin still live in it? Or are you unaware that all of us who were baptized into Christ Jesus were baptized into his death? Therefore we were buried with him by baptism into death, in order that, just as Christ Spirit was raised from the dead by the glory of the Father, so we too may walk in a new way of life. For if we have been joined with him in the likeness of his death, we will certainly also be in the likeness of his resurrection.

Acts 2:38, NASB

Peter said to them, "Repent and be baptized in the name of Jesus Christ for the forgiveness of your sins; and you will receive the gift of the Holy Spirit."

Acts 8:12, NASB
But when they believed Phillip preaching the good news about the kingdom of God and the name of Jesus Christ, they were being baptized, men and women alike.

Spoken to Saul after his conversion; Acts 22:16, NASB
Now why do you delay? Get up and be baptized, and wash away your sins, calling on his name.

Galatians 3:26-27, NIV
You are all sons of God through faith in Christ Jesus, for all of you who were baptized into Christ have clothed yourselves with Christ.

Acts 16:30-33, NIV
He then brought them out and ask, "Sirs, what must I do to be saved?" They replied, "Believe in the Lord Jesus, and you will be saved — you and your household." Then they spoke the word of the Lord to him and to all the others in his house. At that hour of the night the jailer took them and washed their wounds; then immediately he and all his family were baptized.

There are by far too many verses of scripture that refer to baptism to include them all in this book. It seems pretty clear to me that baptism is a necessary part of the Christian conversion, but you will have to make your own decision through your own study. The overall message when every scripture concerning baptism is considered as a whole, without singling out one or two individual verses, is this. To be saved, one must accept that Jesus is the Son of God. Accept him as your personal savior, confess your sins, repent, and be baptized. As Acts 2:38 states that it is after doing this that you will receive the gift of the Holy Spirit. God judges your heart though, and no one can say that not being baptized or not being immersed will exclude you from heaven.

Afterword

There are several more issues that are not necessarily sinful but cause divisions in churches and create separate sects within various denominations. Things like communion, being charismatic, or even worshiping with snakes. Many things cause us to separate ourselves from other Christians in a way that God did not intend. Love God, believe in his Son, accept Jesus as your savior, repent, and be baptized. The good news of the Bible is so much simpler than we make it. My intent was to keep this book short and simple to read. I wanted it to create discussion but not to become a burden. The book is already longer than I intended, so I am choosing to save the discussion on these topics for another day. While I hold out hope that all Christians will read this book to help clarify what they really believe, I suspect that its best use will be for church leadership. I strongly encourage the leadership of every denomination to use this book as a tool for creating some intense debate about why you believe what you do. My belief is that we need to humble ourselves as church leaders and teach nothing but the word of God.

1 Timothy 1:1-11, NASB

As I urged you upon my departure for Macedonia, remain on at Ephesus, in order that you may instruct certain men not to teach strange doctrines, nor to pay attention to myths and endless genealogies, which give rise to mere speculation rather than furthering the administration of God which is by faith. But the goal of our instruction is love from a pure heart and a good conscience and a sincere faith. For some men, straying from these things, have turned aside to fruitless discussion, wanting to be teachers of the law, even though they do not understand what they are saying or the matters about which they make confident assertions. But we all know that the law is good, if one uses it lawfully, realizing the fact that the law is not made for a righteous man, but for those who are lawless and rebellious, for the ungodly and sinners, for the unholy and profane, for those who kill their fathers and mothers, for murderers and immoral men and homosexuals and kidnappers and liars and perjurers, and whatever is contrary to sound teaching, according to the glorious gospel of the blessed God, with which I have been entrusted.

We have been entrusted with the glorious gospel of God. The simple massage is to put our faith in God and to love him with all of our heart. After that, we are to love each other. God expects the rest of the world to know Christians by their obvious love for each other. Our ability to be used by God would be boundless if we were all on the same page.

I would like to give a special thanks to Charlie Jorgenson who kindly did the initial and most difficult edit of this book. He asked me difficult questions and forced me to rethink the statements that I made.

About the Author

Michael W. Freitag is a lifetime Midwesterner. He was born in a small town in South-Central, Illinois, and graduated high school in 1970. After two years of college, he quit to get married and help his wife through nursing school. He never returned to college and spent the next forty years working in a spectroscopy lab, eventually becoming its supervisor. He has been married for more than forty-five years, has three children and eight grandchildren, two who are deceased. Michael pursued his future wife to a local Christian church where they were married. They have attended and served there since that time. He believes in the Ephesians 4:4-6 scripture, which states there is one body, one spirit, one hope, one Lord, one faith, one baptism, one God and Father of all who is over all and through all and in all. God desires his children to be one unified body of believers. The multitude of denominations, divisions, and disunity that we have were not created by God but by man. The unity that God desires will never take place until the teaching of non-scriptural, denominational dogma comes to an end. The Pharisees were severely reprimanded by Jesus for teaching the words and beliefs of men as if they were the words of God. By doing so, they placed a heavy burden on believers. Michael's hope for this book is that it will stimulate every Christian denomination to question what they teach and then to cease teaching anything not God breathed. The death and resurrection of Christ brought an end to salvation through the law, and we must also put an end to making rules and regulations and judging people by them. It's not that hard. Love the Lord with all of your being and love your neighbor as you would yourself.